GENTLE HIKES

Northern Wisconsin's most scenic Lake Superior hikes under 3 miles

Ladona Tornabene, Ph.D., CHES
Melanie Morgan
Lisa Vogelsang, Ph.D.

Adventure Publications, Inc.
Cambridge, MN

ACKNOWLEDGMENTS

Thank you to everyone at the University of Minnesota Duluth (UMD)—especially the Department of Health, Physical Education and Recreation for encouraging us with our second book in this series of health promotion guides. Our gratitude to employees of the following establishments for their assistance with the completion of this book: Pattison, Copper Falls, Big Bay and Amnicon Falls State Parks, Northern Great Lakes Visitor Center, Ashland and Bayfield Chambers of Commerce, 'Mrs. Walking Encyclopedia'—Jan Cameron, City of Superior Parks and Recreation, Superior-Douglas County Visitor Center, Wisconsin Tourist Information Center, Wisconsin Travel Information Center, Wisconsin DNR, Chequamegon-Nicolet National Forest, Brule River State Forest, Bayview Motel (Ashland), Island Inn (Madeline Island) and Seagull Motel (Bayfield).

We thank the following employees at these establishments for copyright permission to use maps: USDA Forest Service and Chequamegon-Nicolet National Forest Service.

Many thanks to Adventure Publications for seeing the initial need for Gentle Hikes and working with us toward the completion of another guide.

We would also like to express deep-felt appreciation to our families and friends for all their support and encouragement.

And last, but certainly not least—The Creator of it all—to whom we give our utmost gratitude. Truly, "The heavens declare the glory of God and the firmament shows and proclaims His handiwork." Ps. 19:1

Please use caution and good sense when participating in outdoor recreational activities. The authors and Adventure Publications, Inc. assume no responsibility for accidents or injuries occurring on the trails, Almost Hikes, waysides, overlooks and picnic areas described in this book.

Learn as much information as you can about the activities and destinations to help prevent accidents and make your recreational experience more enjoyable.

Cover photo by Melanie Morgan: Thimbleberry Nature Trail (pg. 62)
Book design and illustrations by Jonathan Norberg; maps generated by Anthony Hertzel

Copyright 2004 by Ladona Tornabene, Melanie Morgan and Lisa Vogelsang
Adventure Publications, Inc.
820 Cleveland St. S
Cambridge, MN 55008
1-800-678-7006
All rights reserved
Printed in the U.S.A.
ISBN: 1-59193-050-2

DEDICATION

This book is dedicated to the glory of God.
As beautiful as His creation is, it pales in comparison to Him.
It is our hope that you experience both.
Megwich Hchi-Manitou.
Pasa Gweeg!

HELP US KEEP THIS GUIDE UP TO DATE!

Every effort has been made by the authors to make this guide as accurate as possible at press time. However, due to the dynamic nature of trails, etc. we would appreciate your feedback if you find a discrepancy with anything in this book. We would also love to hear your feedback regarding its usefulness to you. Please email Ladona Tornabene ltornabe@d.umn.edu and write 'book feedback' in the subject line. Thank you very much.

TABLE OF CONTENTS

Point Trail/Loop (South) (pg. 110). Photo by Lisa Vogelsang

INTRODUCTION

Gentle Hikes was created out of a desire to share the outdoors with people of all ability levels.

Since this is the second of its kind in a series, we would like to explain how the original concept took form. It actually began on Minnesota's North Shore (which is where our first *Gentle Hikes* book was written) when we asked local merchants: "Do you carry a hiking book that focuses solely on short, relatively easy trails?" Very often, their reply was "Well, not exactly..."

All three authors call Duluth, Minnesota, home and it was the first summer of the new millennium. We had friends and family planning a visit and all of them wanted to go hiking! They wanted to experience scenic beauty via the trails; however, some had very limited time here and some had small children. They needed short hikes. Others had certain physical challenges or were totally new to hiking. They needed easier hikes with specific information about the trails such as inclines, steps and surface type.

We began thinking.

One of the authors has a physical limitation and another is temporarily plagued by sports-related injuries. This, combined with the above, made it clear that we needed to locate easier, shorter trails than those listed in most hiking books. Ideas began to flow and *Gentle Hikes* took form.

Although the term "gentle" is subjective, we have found the topography of Lake Superior's South Shore to be far more gentle than the diverse topography of Minnesota's North Shore. Keep in mind that hiking in the outdoors naturally involves inclines, declines, rocks, roots and uneven terrain. We have created a rating system (pg. 20) describing the extent of these elements so that you may choose a trail compatible with your personal abilities. We have also noted which trails meet Universal Design Standards (in other words, trails that meet accessibility standards for persons of all abilities as opposed to the "average" person). Furthermore, we specify which trails are multi-use, non-motorized paths (i.e. permitting bicyclists and in-line skaters, but prohibiting any motorized vehicles with the exception of motorized wheelchairs).

Whereas most of the trails in this book are well-marked and easy to follow, please be aware that we took the liberty to use parts of existing trails to form our own. We did this in order to meet the *Gentle Hikes* criteria. When this is the case, it's a good idea to familiarize yourself with the trail description to make sure you stay on course.

Whatever your hiking passion—be it continuous Lake Superior views, dramatic waterfalls, breathtaking vistas, rushing rivers, lush wooded paths or paved scenic trails—this book delivers all of these and much more.

Healthy trails to you always!

Ladona Tornabene, Melanie Morgan, Lisa Vogelsang

Ladona Tornabene, Ph.D., CHES, Melanie Morgan, Lisa Vogelsang, Ph.D.

LAYING THE GROUNDWORK

Bay View Trail (pg. 118) in Big Bay State Park on Madeline Island. Photo by Lisa Vogelsang

SUGGESTIONS FOR MAKING YOUR HIKE HAPPIER: CLOTHING & GEAR

Since all of our hikes are less than three miles and are on well-marked trails, we list fewer essentials than other resource guides. Remember to choose trails that are appropriate for your ability and fitness level. Start out slowly and gradually increase your walking speed to a comfortable level, pacing yourself throughout the hike.

Stretch

Stretching before a hike prepares the muscles for activity and stretching after can prevent muscle soreness. Not only does it feel good to stretch, but a flexible muscle is less likely to pull should you move suddenly or accidentally trip.

Rain Gear

We thought we could make it back to the car in time, since it was such a short trail. Lesson learned: always pack a rain jacket! Even though you may start out on a beautiful day, weather conditions can change very quickly. All of us have been caught in rain storms on trails less than a mile long. Waterproof fabrics that are breathable work best for rain gear.

Clothing Fabric Type

There are many choices of clothing fabric in today's market. Wear something breathable that also dries quickly. Cotton feels great on a hot day, but when it gets wet, it stays wet. Newer nylon and blended synthetics are breathable, help wick perspiration away from the skin and dry much faster than cotton.

Head Coverings

Since your head is obviously closest to the sun, it is important to protect the scalp from the sun's burning rays. Many styles of wide brimmed hats and billed caps can be used to offer head protection and shade the eyes. Whatever your style, choose a hat that offers adequate protection from weather conditions and allows for personal comfort.

Sunscreen

Sunscreens are a necessity in preventing sunburns, wrinkles and reducing the risk of skin cancer. Use a waterproof sunscreen with a minimum of SPF 15. Apply before hiking and re-apply about every hour depending upon perspiration levels. Don't forget sunblock for the lips, nose and ears as well as good quality sunglasses to protect your eyes.

Footwear

The shoes and socks you wear can make the difference between an enjoyable outdoor experience or a hike filled with possible blisters and discomfort. Athletic shoes are great for paved or flat trails without many roots or rocks and are appropriate for trails with a Lighter Side of Gentle rating. Sturdier shoes or hiking boots are a good idea for trails with a Moderate or Rugged Side of Gentle rating. When it comes to shoe or boot fit, don't compromise. Purchase your footwear from a merchant who is knowledgeable about hiking and try on the boots with the type of socks you plan to wear on the trail. After purchasing boots or athletic shoes, it is important to break them in prior to hitting the trails.

Cotton socks are not recommended because they absorb moisture and hold it next to your skin, which may cause blisters or cold feet. Synthetics or other natural fiber socks that are thick or made specifically for hiking are ideal. Some people prefer using a liner sock as well to ensure comfort and reduce the risk of blisters.

The Big Stick

There are several styles of hiking sticks and poles available. Many types have been shown to improve balance and reduce the risk of knee or ankle injury. They are especially useful on declines, inclines and uneven terrain. There are advantages and disadvantages within styles as well as between poles and sticks. If you are considering using a stick or pole, do some homework and talk to local merchants who carry such items. Keep in mind that although most poles are adjustable and some have shock absorption capabilities, their tips can damage tree roots. Hiking sticks are not adjustable and may be heavier to carry, but cause less damage to roots. Whichever you choose, being knowledgeable about proper usage is a must for your safety and the well-being of the environment.

Bug Beaters

Mosquitoes, black flies, gnats, biting flies, ticks, chiggers and sand fleas are all realities to consider when going outdoors. Prevent yourself from being the main course for the bugs' supper by testing which repellent works best for you. Some people swear by a natural soap product called Northwoods Suds. Others like Herbal Armor as a natural remedy. Whether you go natural or traditional, we recommend a product that is healthy for you and the environment. Remember to use repellent on clothing as well as exposed skin. During times of high foliage it is recommended that you wear pants tucked into your socks to prevent tick and other beastie bites. Also check yourself for ticks after any trek into the woods, and know how to remove embedded ticks. Know the signs and symptoms of Lyme disease.

Water

Drink whether thirsty or not because if you wait until you are thirsty, you are already dehydrated. A good rule of thumb is to bring 8 ounces (1 cup) of water for each 15 minutes of hiking expected. The Superior Hiking Trail Association (Two Harbors, MN) and other sources recommend allowing 1 hour for every 1.5 to 3 miles of trail covered. Since all of our trails are less than three miles, this means taking a minimum of 32 oz. of water with you (more on a hot day).

Sports drinks are OK, but soft drinks are not recommended, nor are any beverages containing caffeine or alcohol because you will lose more fluid than contained in the drinks. Do not drink water from streams, rivers or lakes unless you have a water purification device to clean the water of bacteria and other impurities.

Snacks

Bring food on hikes lasting longer than an hour. Suggested snack items include dried fruits, crackers, granola, cereal, energy bars and trail mixes. To help keep trails beautiful, pack out anything you take in.

Safety Items

A readily accessible, genuine survival whistle is a necessity even on short hikes. The volume and pitch can scare away unwanted animals or alert others of your position in an emergency. Other items not previously mentioned that we recommend bringing along are personal identification, a small first aid kit, trail maps/descriptions and a small flashlight.

Fun Items

While experiencing the spectacular scenic beauty of these trails, a camera and plenty of film or memory cards is an essential! If there's one bug we actually want to bite you, it's the shutterbug! Compact binoculars are also fun to have for identifying birds and butterflies. A small pocket notebook and pen are also nice for recording memories or thoughts.

Daypacks

Backpacks or waist packs are suggested and needed when carrying water or more than one pound of gear. Models with pockets especially for water bottles are convenient. The kind of pack needed depends on the type of hiking you'll be doing, how much gear you plan to carry and its comfort and functionality.

Conclusion

When out on the trail away from modern conveniences, an ounce of prevention is worth more than a pound of cure. Some say it's worth a pound of gold! Implementing the above suggestions may take a little planning and organizing initially, but you'll be glad you brought that pack along.

TRAILS

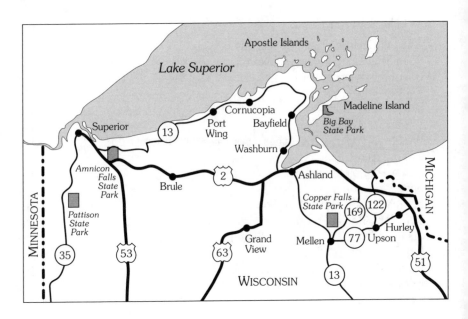

AUTHORS' CORNER

Best Lake Superior views:

Best waterfalls:

Best vistas:

* Meets Universal Design Standards

Best wooded trails:

Best river views:

Best lake views (other than Superior):

Best harbor views:

* Meets Universal Design Standards

Best interpretive trails:

Flattest trails:

* Meets Universal Design Standards

Paved trails:

Off the beaten path:

* Meets Universal Design Standards

Big Bay Town Park Trail (pg. 128). Photo by Lisa Vogelsang

TRAIL USAGE INFORMATION

The following is general information pertaining to the majority of trails in this book. For specific questions regarding any particular trail, please contact respective trail headquarters (phone number provided after Trailhead Directions & Parking listed on all hikes in this section or see Appendix B).

State Park Trails:

We have included four of Wisconsin's State Parks in this book: Amnicon Falls, Pattison, Big Bay and Copper Falls. These parks offer numerous hiking trails. Not only have we featured some of the established trails, but have strung together pathways to create loops or out-and-back treks to provide the most scenic routes we could find within the *Gentle Hikes* criteria (pg. 20).

Certain state parks have multi-use trails (check with individual parks for maps or pick up a copy of *Wisconsin State Parks* by Bill Bailey). Although some parks have designated ATV/snowmobile trails, motorized vehicles are prohibited on all state park hiking trails. Electric wheelchairs are permitted on all state park hiking trails.

In addition to quality hiking trails, Wisconsin State Parks offer many amenities. Contact the state parks listed in this book or the Wisconsin Department of Natural Resources (1-608-266-2621 or www.dnr.state.wi.us).

North Country National Scenic Trail (NCNST) Sections:

Putting footprints onto dreams, the NCTA (North Country Trail Association) is working closely with the National Park Service to complete the longest National Scenic Trail in the United States. When finished, its length will total over 4,000 miles! Named one of the 16 National Millennium Trails by the White House Millennium Council, the NCNST spans seven states (North Dakota, Minnesota, Wisconsin, Upper and Lower Michigan, Ohio, Pennsylvania and New York). At the time of writing (October, 2003), more than 1,700 miles were completed and certified. In Wisconsin, the NCNST has thus far completed a 61-mile stretch through the northern half of the Chequamegon-Nicolet National Forest.

Designated as a hiking trail, the NCTA discourages horse use as well as mountain biking. Mountain bikes may not be ridden where the trail crosses wilderness areas. Motorized use on the trail is prohibited under the existing Forest Off-Road Vehicle Policy.

The NCTA is a nonprofit organization that relies primarily on volunteers to build and maintain the trail. Their national headquarters is located at 229 E. Main Street, Lowell, Michigan 49331. For more information please contact the North Country Trail Association at 1-888-454-NCTA or www.northcountrytrail.org. When reported and available, trail conditions are posted on their website as well.

Osaugie, Millennium, Brownstone, Washburn and Ashland Bayfront Trails:

These trails' round trip distances pushed or exceeded our criteria. Therefore, we divided those trails into sections*, each with distinct turn-around points.

In each section of the trails we showcase their unique attributes, provide entrance access from the closest parking areas and provide various distances, which makes it convenient to hike a single section or string them together for a longer walk. Although many sections are paved, none except the Millennium Trail meet Universal Design Standards. For information on potential wheelchair accessibility, see pg. 206.

In addition to these trails, the cities therein offer many amenities. See Appendix A under vacation planning for respective listings.

*Please note that we did not include the entire Osaugie Trail as sections of it came literally within feet of the parallel ATV trail.

Osaugie Trail: Round trip distance of this predominately paved path is 10 miles; therefore, we divided it into three sections. Sights on this trail include the busiest harbor on the Great Lakes; the world's only remaining whaleback ship; the Richard I. Bong Heritage Center; Barker's Island; historic Fairlawn Mansion and some very picturesque nature areas.

Millennium Trail: Round trip distance of this predominately paved path is 3.6 miles; therefore, we divided it into two sections. Both sections meet Universal Design Standards, are very flat and pass through the second-to-largest municipal forest located within a city (Superior) in the United States!

Brownstone Trail: Round trip distance of this trail is just under three miles so we could have included it as one, but opted to divide it into two sections. Its spurs lead to a hotel and a restaurant. Stringing these sections together at time of writing (July, 2003) was blocked by a partial trail closure due to severe erosion. Sights on this trail include scenic views of Lake Superior and lush wooded areas.

Washburn Walking Trail: Round trip distance of this trail is 2.7 miles so we could have included it as one, but opted to divide it into two sections. Both sections offer beautiful views of Lake Superior's Chequamegon Bay and one section indicates wheelchair accessibility although it does not currently meet Universal Design Standards.

Ashland Bayfront Trail: The entire Ashland Bayfront Trail is part of a comprehensive long-range waterfront development plan that has involved Ashland's community as well as several agencies and businesses over the past two decades. The commitment to enhance publicly usable space along the waterfront continues as a testament to the pride this community takes in showcasing its Bayfront!

Round trip distance of this predominately paved path is 7 miles; therefore, we divided it into five sections. An outstanding feature of all sections is the interpretive markers. These contain well-researched information about the history of Ashland and Chequamegon Bay, timber mills, shipping, electricity, area wildlife, Lake Superior and more! When visiting, we recommend allowing plenty of time so you can read them all. Furthermore, the trail offers many unobstructed views of Lake Superior's Chequamegon Bay and a beach area.

Brule River State Forest:

The 42,000-acre forest is used by more diverse species of mammals and birds than virtually any other northern Wisconsin acreage of similar size! Two of the three designated hiking trails met our Gentle Hikes criteria and are featured in this book (Stony Hill Nature Trail pg. 66 & Historical Bayfield Road Trail pg. 68). Stony Hill features a very large white pine measuring 11' in circumference and the Historical Bayfield contains an extraordinary area of northern hardwoods—the only one of its kind in the entire Brule River State Forest!

Pet Policies:

This is not a conclusive list of pet policies for all trails in this book. For more information, call the phone number listed at the beginning of a specific trail.

General Information: Please pick up after your pet at all times. Wherever dogs are permitted, they must be kept on an 8' or shorter leash at all times.

State Park Trails: By state law, pets are not allowed on beaches, in picnic areas, playgrounds, buildings or on nature or ski trails. However, Pattison State Park has a designated Dog Trail. We feature part of this Dog Trail (see pg. 52) but recommend you pick up a map from the park office as well. Copper Falls State Park allows dogs on the Red Granite Falls Trail.

In all state parks pets are allowed in camp areas, on roads and in other areas of the park that are not developed for public use.

North Country National Scenic Trail (NCNST) Sections: The sections of the NCNST featured in this book require all pets to be leashed.

Osaugie, Millennium, Brownstone, Washburn and Ashland Bayfront Trails: Pets must be leashed.

Brule River State Forest: Pets are not permitted in buildings, picnic areas, nature or ski trails. However, they are permitted in campgrounds and must be on a leash no longer than 8'.

Trail Closures:

Generally trails remain open for hiking until snow season begins. Trail reroutings, wildlife habitats, and/or hunting season could potentially close certain trails. Please check with contact listed on every trail regarding closures.

When Snowflakes Fly:

No trails are plowed during snow season, with the following exceptions: Pattison State Park plows the Big Manitou Falls Almost Hike (from parking area through wheelchair accessible portion) during snow season and it is sometimes sanded. The Park also plows the path from the main parking area/office to the Shelter as well as from the exercise equipment to the lake (which serves as an ice rink).

Amnicon plows the road to the office and to the covered bridge.

Big Manitou Falls at Pattison State Park (pg. 155). Photo by Lisa Vogelsang

HOW TO USE THIS GUIDE
Trail Rating:

To accommodate hikers of all levels, each trail follows a rating system. The rating system is governed by a set of criteria (see below) and offers three levels. Trails range from the Lighter Side of Gentle which includes all paved trails (and more) to the Rugged Side of Gentle which offers more challenge to those who desire it. The Moderate Side of Gentle, as you might expect, falls somewhere in between. All trails are under 3 miles in total length.

Regardless of the rating, each trail will always state the trail surface and width, number of inclines over 10 degrees, steepest and longest incline, safety concerns and all step and bench locations.

Our trail descriptions are very detailed and correspond to the trail in increments of tenths of a mile. We have made every attempt to locate and note trail aspects that may challenge some (e.g., inclines, rocks, roots, steps, etc.) as well as features that may be helpful (e.g., benches, handrailings, paved trails, etc.). With this information, each person can make an informed decision based on his/her abilities as to how far to go on a certain trail or choose another altogether.

Icons:

The following icons represent our trail rating system.

 The Lighter Side of Gentle must meet all of the following criteria (excluding options):

Inclines: 10-12° (or less)
Rock/Root: Minimal (intermittent moderate sections)
Total number of steps encountered throughout the trail: <25
Trail surface: Even (intermittent uneven sections)

 The Moderate Side of Gentle meets ONE or more of the following criteria:

Inclines: 14-16° (or no more than 2 inclines between 18-22°, not exceeding 35' in length)
Rock/Root: Moderate
Total number of steps encountered throughout the trail: <175
Trail surface: Even or uneven

 The Rugged Side of Gentle meets ONE or more of the following criteria:

Inclines: 18-22°
Rock/Root: Moderate to Significant
Total number of steps encountered throughout the trail: <325
Trail surface: Even or uneven, laid log paths possible.

Icons in the Descriptions:

These icons, embedded in the trail description and mileage section for each trail, allow you to quickly see what's ahead on the trail.

 Inclines: Indicates the location of the steepest incline on the trail.

Steps: We note in the description if they ascend/descend, their composition and if they have handrails or not. Non-continuous indicates a brief resting area between sets of steps.

 Benches: Indicates the location of benches on the trail.

 Photo opportunities: On our trails we have chosen places where we thought the views were photo worthy. Some are obvious, others are purely subjective; we think you will be pleased with our suggestions. We have found it to be a great way of preserving and sharing memories for years to come.

Maps:

Provided for each trail, maps show mileage markers that correspond to selected trail descriptions. Not all mileage markers are shown on the maps, only those that will help you locate your position on the trail.

Other Items You'll Find:

 Foot Note:

Information that may be of interest or inspiration to our readers, including nearby sites to see. These are listed on the specific trail, Almost Hike, wayside or picnic area to which they pertain.

 SAYS WHO?

Professional information from reputable sources related to health education issues. These are scattered throughout the book.

*An asterisk means that the trail has been given a Gentle Hikes name because no name previously existed or it is part of another trail.

Location • The State of Wisconsin does not use mile markers on U.S. 2 or WI 13. Therefore, mileage on U.S. 2 is given as follows: From the Superior-Douglas County Visitors Center (305 Harbor View Parkway, Superior, WI) on the west and the Wisconsin Travel Information Center in Hurley (1200 10th Ave N., Hurley, WI) on the east. Mileage on WI 13 is given from the Superior-Douglas County Visitors Center (305 Harbor View Parkway, Superior, WI) and the intersection of U.S. 2 and WI 13 west of Ashland.

• **Trail Highlights: Though subjective, we believe that these highlights give an account of the sights you can expect to see.**

TRAILHEAD DIRECTIONS & PARKING:

Directions are listed from U.S. 2 or WI 13 at the point of turnoff from these roads. Mileage is given for the purpose of proper navigation.

TRAILHEAD FACILITIES & FEES:

Unless otherwise noted, facilities are mentioned only if they are at trailhead parking area or on the trail. Fees pertain to parking and entrance. All Wisconsin state parks in this guide as well as some other locations (see individual trail description) require a use permit to enter. Day use or annual permits are available at state park offices, headquarters or self-pay boxes.

TOTAL TRAIL LENGTH, SURFACE & WIDTH:

Trail length is round trip distance to the nearest tenth of a mile. Trail surface varies from paved, gravel and hardpacked dirt to rock and root. When rock and root are present, they are reported in three categories: minimum, moderate and significant. Please note: paved trails are not plowed or de-iced during the snow season with the exception of Pattison State Park (see Trail Usage Info, pg. 16).

INCLINES & ALERTS:

Although inclines can be reported as % grade, we chose to use degrees (for conversion table, see Appendix C). The number of inclines exceeding 10° (18% grade), their degree ranges, the steepest incline (its length and location) and the longest incline (exceeding 30') is listed for every trail. Alerts include potential safety hazards or other matters of concern.

CONTACT:

For more information about the trail, state park or area, get in touch with this organization.

MILEAGE & DESCRIPTION:

This is your step-by-step description of what you'll encounter on the trail. Not every tenth of a mile is included, usually only those that help you locate your position on the trail or that offer amenities, potential challenges or spectacular views.

Big Bay Town Park Lagoon (pg. 169) in Big Bay State Park on Madeline Island. Photo by Melanie Morgan

Superior • Off U.S. 2, 4 miles from Superior-Douglas County Visitor Center

- **Very flat trail ideally suited for non-motorized activities.**
- **Numerous opportunities for wildlife viewing and animal track identification.**

TRAILHEAD DIRECTIONS & PARKING:

From the Superior-Douglas County Visitor Center, head west on U.S. 2 for 1.7 miles. At Tower Ave (WI 35) turn left (south) and travel 1 mile to 28th Street. Turn right (west) and travel 0.9 mile to sign for Superior Forest Ski Trails. Turn left into paved parking lot.

TRAILHEAD FACILITIES & FEES:

Portable toilet, table, grill. No fees for trail use during non-ski season.

TOTAL TRAIL LENGTH, SURFACE & WIDTH:

0.9 mile; paved; 10' wide and constructed to meet the standards for Universal Design (see pg. 207 for additional information).

INCLINES & ALERTS:

There are no inclines greater than 10°. This is a multi-use, non-motorized path and may be used by in-line skaters and cyclists.

CONTACT:

City of Superior Parks and Recreation: (715) 395-7270

MILEAGE & DESCRIPTION

0.0   Trailhead begins at Millennium Trail sign at west end of parking lot. Follow around parking area to east entrance. If you like looking for animal tracks, we recommend that you take along a field guide for identification. This trail passes through marshlands.

0.5   Elmira Street signals end of east extension. Turn around and retrace path to trailhead.

0.9   Trailhead.

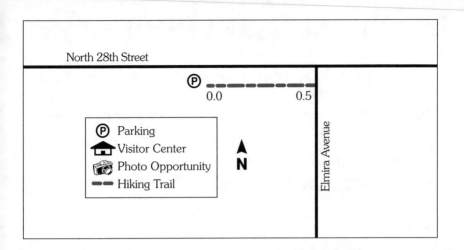

 SAYS WHO?

Concerned about osteoporosis?

Walk briskly. Women who exercise have a lower risk of developing osteoporosis.

Harvard Women's Health Watch [6]

 # MILLENNIUM TRAIL (WEST)

Superior • Off U.S. 2, 4 miles from Superior-Douglas County Visitor Center

- **Very flat trail ideally suited for non-motorized activities through quiet woods of mixed forest.**
- **Trail runs through second-largest municipal forest located within a city in the United States.**

TRAILHEAD DIRECTIONS & PARKING:
From the Superior-Douglas County Visitor Center, head west on U.S. 2 for 1.7 miles. At Tower Ave (WI 35) turn left (south) and travel 1 mile to 28th Street. Turn right (west) and travel 0.9 mile to sign for Superior Forest Ski Trails. Turn left into paved parking lot.

TRAILHEAD FACILITIES & FEES:
Portable toilet, table, grill. No fees for trail use during non-ski season.

TOTAL TRAIL LENGTH, SURFACE & WIDTH:
2.7 miles; paved; 10' wide and constructed to meet the standards for Universal Design (see pg. 207 for additional information).

INCLINES & ALERTS:
There are no inclines greater than 10°. This is a multi-use, non-motorized path and may be used by in-line skaters and cyclists.

CONTACT:
City of Superior Parks and Recreation: (715) 395-7270

MILEAGE & DESCRIPTION

0.0 Trailhead begins at Millennium Trail sign at west end of parking lot on 10'-wide paved path. There are six benches on this trail located approximately 1000' apart with pavement running up to and under each.

0.2 At stop sign, turn right and continue on paved path.

0.7 Unique boardwalk made of recycled plastic extends over marsh area. This is a great place to look for animal tracks in the mud. If you enjoy this type of activity, we recommend that you take along a field guide for identification. Trail continues to meander through the forest.

Although we typically do not identify wildflowers on our trails since they vary as to season hiked, this one is noteworthy. This is the only trail on which we observed Northern Sweet Coltsfoot in such abundance (a photo can be seen in the field guide *What's Doin' the Bloomin'?*). It is a very early bloomer in the spring and if you see it once it has gone to seed it will look like a pretty puffy weed!

1.4 Once you reach Billings Drive, this marks the end of the trail. Turn around and retrace path to trailhead.

2.7   Trailhead.

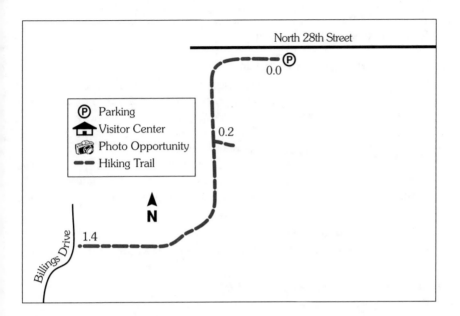

 SAYS WHO?

Feeling blue? Get into the green.

Walking for 30 minutes 4-6 days per week at a moderate pace can help to prevent or reduce depression.

Exercising Your Way to Better Mental Health [44,42,43,27,25,26]

RIVERFRONT TRAIL

Superior • Off U.S. 2, 4 miles from Superior-Douglas County Visitor Center

---

• **Spectacular St. Louis Bay views!**

TRAILHEAD DIRECTIONS & PARKING:

From the Superior-Douglas County Visitor Center, head east on U.S. 2 for 1.7 miles. At Tower Ave (WI 35) turn left (south) and travel 0.5 mile to 21st Street. Turn right (west) and travel 1.6 miles to sign for Billings Park; drive around traffic circle to Billings Drive. Turn right and continue to next Billings Park sign and arrow pointing to the right. Turn here and drive to small paved lot at end of indrive. Parking is also allowed on one side of drive—please note signs. Although there are many access points to this trail, we chose this one as it was near designated parking. Do not park at boat launch (passed as you entered the park) as it is permit and wheelchair accessible parking only.

TRAILHEAD FACILITIES & FEES:

Flush toilets, water spigot (see Billings Park Picnic Area pg. 185). No fees for trail use.

TOTAL TRAIL LENGTH, SURFACE & WIDTH:

0.7 mile; paved; average 10' wide.

INCLINES & ALERTS:

There are no inclines greater than 10°; however, trail access is not flat. This is a multi-use non-motorized path.

CONTACT:

City of Superior Parks and Recreation: (715) 395-7270

MILEAGE & DESCRIPTION

0.0 Trailhead begins at steps to the left of redwood fence. Descend 51 steps (cement, double handrail, non-continuous). Turn right at base of steps onto 10' paved path. Immediately you will be treated to fabulous views of St. Louis Bay.

0.1 There are two benches in this section that provide a relaxing way to take in the wonderful views of the Bay.

0.2 A picnic table here makes a fine spot for dining in a grassy area right along the Bay.

0.3 Ascend 58 steps (cement, partial double handrail, non-continuous) that take you into Billings Park Picnic Area and through a fully accessible playground for individuals with disabilities. This is a truly unique feature! At intersection near park road, follow pavement to the left. Continue toward park entrance.

0.4 Near park entrance, look across entrance road for 10'-wide paved path (at time of writing path was barricaded but open to foot traffic). Use caution when crossing park road and access trail at barricade. This will eventually take you back to the steps where you began the trail.

0.5 Another bench affords a picturesque view. The nearby bridge leads to a tiny island frequented by geese and other waterfowl.

0.6 Take some time for relaxing and soaking in the spectacular bay views on this strategically placed bench. When you're ready, retrace path to trailhead and parking area.

0.7 Trailhead.

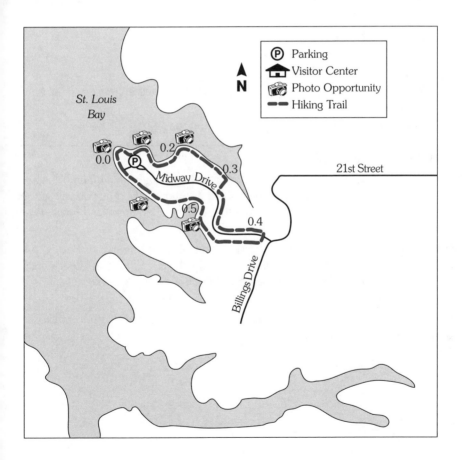

BARKER'S ISLAND TRAIL*

Superior • Off U.S. 2, 0.1 mile from Superior-Douglas County Visitor Center • *Gentle Hikes name

---

• **Exceptional views of Superior Bay and the hills of Duluth.**

TRAILHEAD DIRECTIONS & PARKING:
From U.S. 2 at the Superior-Douglas County Visitor Center, turn east onto service road beside Visitor Center and Bong WWII Heritage Center. Follow signs indicating Barker's Island. Continue to paved parking area near *SS Meteor*. Designated wheelchair accessible parking (RV spaces available at Visitor Center lot).

TRAILHEAD FACILITIES & FEES:
Flush toilets (located in the *SS Meteor* but has same hours as gift shops), portable toilet (seasonal), water fountain, playground, picnic area (see Barker's Island Play Area Picnic pg. 184). No fees for trail use.

TOTAL TRAIL LENGTH, SURFACE & WIDTH:
1.0 mile; paved; average 8' wide.

INCLINES & ALERTS:
No inclines greater than 10°. Trail nears Barker's Island entrance road at times.

CONTACT:
Superior-Douglas County Visitor Center: (800) 942-5313

MILEAGE & DESCRIPTION

0.0   Trailhead begins at southeast corner of parking area behind green billboard for Meteor Museum and Charter Fishing directionals. Shortly you will see several picnic areas to the right across the road (see Barker's Island Picnic Area pg. 184 for more information).

0.3   A slight decline signals the welcome, beautiful views of Superior Bay as the remainder of the trail hugs this scenic body of water. If here in late summer, expect rows of common tansies to line the trail adding a wonderful splash of golden color.

0.5   Pavement ends as does the trail. Turn around and retrace path to trailhead. Expect marvelous views of the hills of Duluth on return.

1.0   Trailhead.

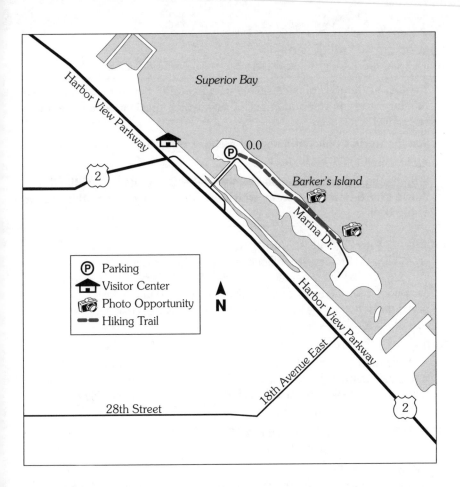

Map legend:
- (P) Parking
- Visitor Center
- Photo Opportunity
- Hiking Trail

Labels on map: Superior Bay, Harbor View Parkway, 2, 0.0, Barker's Island, Marina Dr., Harbor View Parkway, 2, 18th Avenue East, 28th Street, N

🦉 SAYS WHO?

More is better—when it comes to brains, that is!

Individuals who maintain their aerobic fitness have been shown to preserve more brain tissue density as they age.

Journals of Gerontology Series A: Biological Sciences & Medical Sciences [32]

OSAUGIE TRAIL

Superior Bay to Trail Beginning
Superior • Off U.S. 2, 0.1 mile from Superior-Douglas County Visitor Center

- **The City of Duluth's hillside serves as a beautiful backdrop against spectacular sweeping views of Superior Bay, which sports a wide variety of waterfowl.**

- **See the world's only remaining whaleback ship, the** SS *Meteor,* **which was built in Superior in 1896.**

- **Stop by the Superior-Douglas County Visitor Center as well as the Bong World War II Heritage Center, which are housed together on this section of the trail.**

TRAILHEAD DIRECTIONS & PARKING:
From U.S. 2 at the Superior-Douglas County Visitor Center, turn east onto service road beside Visitor Center and Bong WWII Heritage Center. Parking is available on service road, or follow sign indicating Barker's Island. Continue to paved parking area. Designated wheelchair accessible parking (RV spaces available at Visitor Center lot).

TRAILHEAD FACILITIES & FEES:
Portable toilet (seasonal) located at east end of parking lot within wooden enclosure. Flush toilets (wheelchair accessible) and water located nearby in Visitor Center. Picnic tables and playground in Harbor View Park outside of Visitor Center. No fees for trail use.

TOTAL TRAIL LENGTH, SURFACE & WIDTH:
0.8 mile; paved; average 10' wide.

INCLINES & ALERTS:
No inclines greater than 10°. This section is a multi-use non-motorized path.

CONTACT:
City of Superior Parks and Recreation: (715) 395-7270

MILEAGE & DESCRIPTION

0.0 Trailhead begins at northwest corner of parking area near observation/fishing deck on 20'-wide paved path. From parking lot, turn left onto trail (trail continues to the right; see Superior Bay to Old Stockade Site, pg. 36). Immediately to the right are several strategically placed benches serving up tranquil views of Superior Bay, which sports a wide variety of waterfowl. Look for the SS *Meteor*—the only remaining whaleback ship in the world!

Path narrows to 8' as it continues to deliver breathtaking views of the bay for the remainder of this trail. The hill you see to the west is the City of Duluth. Look right approximately 20' prior to bridge for some beautiful rocks on the waterfront. Cross bridge (paved, double handrail).

0.1 Three more benches provide gorgeous bay views as well as mark a trail inter-section. The paved spur to the left leads to two entities housed within the same establishment. The Superior-Douglas County Visitor Center is staffed and well-stocked with useful information for the traveler. The Bong World War II Heritage Center is a tribute to the efforts of a nation in the defense of freedom. Whether you visit now or later, we deem it a very worthwhile stop. Additionally, this area is home to Harbor View Park, which boasts two very nice playground areas and several picnic tables.

To stay on the trail, continue straight ahead. This will take you to the very beginning of the Osaugie Trail, officially marked with its signature archway. Another bench en route hosts the Superior Bay view.

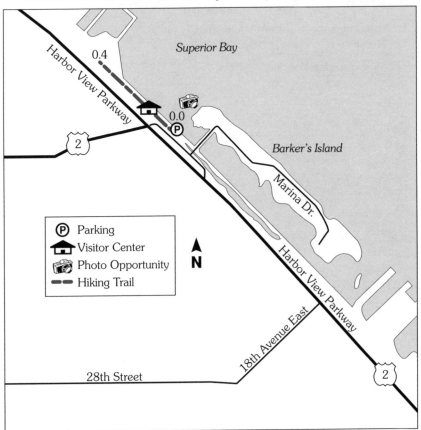

0.4 The end of the pavement signals the end of this section of the trail. Beyond this is Conners Point, which is an industrial park, so we do not advise hiking any further. As previously mentioned, the Osaugie originates from this loca-tion and as you retrace the path to trailhead, you will actually be starting from the official trail beginning.

0.8 Trailhead.

Foot Note:

The Bong World War II Heritage Center houses exhibits, interactive displays, a fully restored P-38 plane, Educational Video Theatre, flight simulators and stories of how ordinary people became extraordinary heroes. For more information contact (888)-816-WWII or www.bongheritagecenter.org.

 SAYS WHO?

Have a family history of cancer, heart disease, or type 2 diabetes and want to reduce your risk?

Regular walking has been shown to significantly reduce the risks of these and other chronic diseases.

New England Journal of Medicine [3,4,6,12,15,19,23]

OSAUGIE TRAIL

Superior Bay to Old Stockade Site

Superior • Off U.S. 2, 0.1 mile from Superior-Douglas County Visitor Center

- **Location of the Lake Superior Dragon Boat Festival.**
- **Spectacular views of Barker's Island Harbor.**
- **See Superior's "treasured jewel," the 1890 Fairlawn Mansion.**

TRAILHEAD DIRECTIONS & PARKING:

From U.S. 2 at the Superior-Douglas County Visitor Center, turn east onto service road beside Visitor Center and Bong WWII Heritage Center. Parking is available on service road, or follow sign indicating Barker's Island. Continue to paved parking area. Designated wheelchair accessible parking (RV spaces available at Visitor Center lot).

TRAILHEAD FACILITIES & FEES:

Portable toilet (seasonal) located at east end of parking lot within wooden enclosure. Flush toilets (wheelchair accessible) and water located nearby in Visitor Center. Picnic tables and playground in Harbor View Park outside of Visitor Center. No fees for trail use.

TOTAL TRAIL LENGTH, SURFACE & WIDTH:

1.8 mile; paved; average 10' wide.

INCLINES & ALERTS:

No inclines greater than 10°. This section is a multi-use non-motorized path. There are two road crossings—use caution.

CONTACT:

City of Superior Parks and Recreation: (715) 395-7270

MILEAGE & DESCRIPTION

0.0 Trailhead begins at east corner of parking area near pond with water fountains on 10'-wide paved path. From parking lot, turn right onto trail (trail continues to the left; see Superior Bay to Trail Beginning, pg. 32). To the left is the *SS Meteor*, the only remaining whaleback ship in the world!

Pass under the Osaugie Trail signature arch. At trail intersection, turn right (left takes you to Barker's Island Trail, see pg. 30). The fountain pond makes a picturesque site with Superior Bay and the City of Duluth as a backdrop.

0.1 Alert: Trail crosses two-lane entrance road—use caution. The remainder of this trail takes on more traffic noise as it parallels U.S. 2 but still provides enough green space to give the feeling of being on a trail. The two benches in this section provide nice views of Superior Bay and to the distant north, the hills of Duluth.

0.2 Alert: Trail crosses entrance road to Barker's Island. Use caution as vehicles may be entering from U.S. 2 or exiting the island.

0.3 We think this bench should be double-sided. It affords a nice view of a beach area on Barker's Island (see Barker's Island Picnic Area, pg. 184) in front of you, but wait until you turn around. Behind you is Superior's "treasured jewel," the 1890 Fairlawn Mansion and Museum, which is beautiful in its own right.

0.4 This bench overlooks the site of the Lake Superior Dragon Boat Festival, held during the third week every August. All proceeds from the race go to aid charities that Twin Ports Rotary Clubs help support.

0.5 Two more benches in this section offer marsh and Barker's Island Marina views.

0.7 Two more benches in this section provide marina views. As you continue on the trail, views of the marina get better.

0.8 These next two benches make "getting benched" a beautiful thing. The first serves up incredible marina views with numerous species of waterfowl making it a "must sit." The second would win "Bench of the Trail" award if such a competition existed. Spectacular marina views with the hills of Duluth serving as a backdrop merit our photo op stamp of approval—especially at dusk.

0.9 A caution sign signals a trail intersection in 80', a slight decline and uneven pavement. Veer right at this intersection and head toward gazebo. Notice the time capsule to the right and further on, a marker for the Old Stockade Site. Take some time to read about the Summer of 1862 and the history of this site. Note: Trail does continue (see Old Stockade Site to Loonsfoot Landing, pg. 40); however, to complete this section, turn around and retrace path to trailhead.

1.8 Trailhead

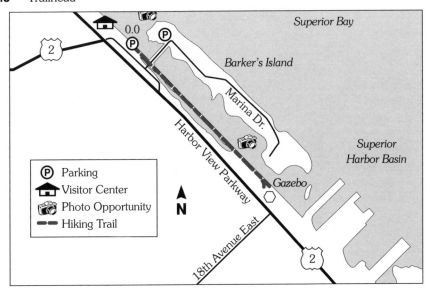

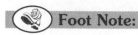 **Foot Note:**

The Fairlawn Mansion is an award-winning 42-room Victorian Museum. Built in 1890, it is one of America's castles and is open year-round for guided tours. For more information call (715) 394-5712 or www.fairlawn.org.

 SAYS WHO?

Want to improve your immunity? Walk briskly around your community!

Regular moderate exercise such as brisk walking can improve immunity by increasing white blood cells (WBC). Walking a short time can increase WBC for one to two hours and walking over 30 minutes can increase WBC production for over 24 hours!

The Physician and Sportsmedicine [24]

OSAUGIE TRAIL

Old Stockade Site to Loonsfoot Landing
Superior • On U.S. 2, 1 mile from Superior-Douglas County Visitor Center

- **Path leads through a marsh area that is very picturesque and known for wildlife sightings.**

TRAILHEAD DIRECTIONS & PARKING:
From U.S. 2 at the Superior-Douglas County Visitor Center, drive southeast 1 mile to traffic lights at 18th Avenue E. Turn toward the bay and brown Historical Marker into paved parking area. Designated wheelchair accessible parking available.

TRAILHEAD FACILITIES & FEES:
Gazebo and picnic tables, historical marker. No fees for trail use.

TOTAL TRAIL LENGTH, SURFACE & WIDTH:
2.4 miles; paved; average 10' wide.

INCLINES & ALERTS:
No inclines greater than 10°. This section is a multi-use non-motorized path. Asphalt is uneven throughout entire trail with some overgrowth possible in summer. There are two road crossings and a railroad crossing—use caution.

CONTACT:
City of Superior Parks and Recreation: (715) 395-7270

MILEAGE & DESCRIPTION

0.0 Trailhead begins near gazebo at sign indicating Old Stockade Site. Take some time to read about the Summer of 1862 and the history of this site. From sign, access lower 10' paved path closer to the water and turn right (trail continues to the left; see Superior Bay to Old Stockade Site, pg. 36). The first bench you encounter will be on grassy surface and doesn't appear to be part of the trail as all other benches are directly on the path with paved access. We speculate that this one is part of the wayside, but nonetheless offers a nice view of Superior Bay. The very first intersection to the right leads back to the parking area. Continue straight and pass under the Osaugie Trail signature arch.

This bench is officially part of the Osaugie Trail and offers a nice view of Barker's Island Marina to the left; straight ahead is Superior Bay as well as the lovely homes on the Island.

0.1 Alert: Stop sign on trail at intersection. Cross service road and wayside entry drive—use caution. This section brings you closer to U.S. 2 but only for approximately 0.1 mile. Soon you will find a trail marker to the left. Continue straight. Find another bench that offers a partial view of the Bay. The dock to the right was inactive at time of writing (August 2003).

0.2 Sign indicating steep grade; however, it does not exceed 10°. Trail takes on a more secluded feel as it turns away from U.S. 2 and passes through a wooded area.

0.3 You will pass under another Osaugie Trail signature arch as the trail turns back toward U.S. 2.

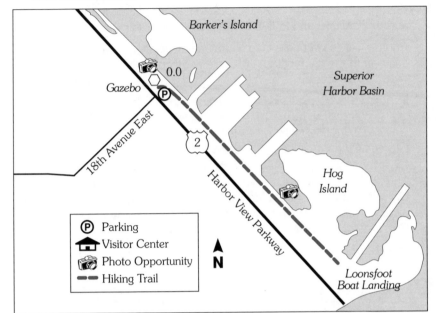

0.4 Alert: Stop sign on trail at intersection. In 100' trail crosses service road and then an active railroad. When crossing railroad be aware that remote control locomotives operate in this area and may be unoccupied—use caution. The pavement ends for approximately 50' then resumes under next Osaugie Trail signature arch.

0.5 Once again trail turns away from U.S. 2 and offers views of Superior Bay to the left.

0.6 Bench affords opportunity to listen for a variety of bird calls in this semi-wooded setting.

0.7 Simply a great location for another bench, and it's worth the stop. Picturesque views of the bay framed by trees and shrubs make it easy to forget you're in the middle of town. Pass under Osaugie Trail signature arch.

0.8 Bridge (wood, double handrail) with nice views of inland bay to the left. This is a very pretty spot in and of itself, but plan to spend some time here as wildlife has been seen. If you visit in late summer, expect a plethora of common tansies. A bench further on provides lovely views of marsh with much bird activity.

Another pass under the signature arch leads to an intersection that is an ATV gravel crossing. Use caution and pick up paved path straight ahead.

0.9 This intersection has a sign indicating East End Neighborhood, a 0.5 mile trail to the right taking you precisely to that neighborhood. Loonsfoot Landing and Tri-County Corridor to left; turn left. Trail passes directly behind private property. Please be respectful and stay on trail. To the left are some very scenic views of the bay inlet and an active site for waterfowl.

1.0 Bench with views of an inactive dock and Duluth hillside to the left; straight ahead is bay inlet and to the right is Loonsfoot Landing.

1.1 Another bench overlooks the picturesque marsh area. In approximately 400' find sign to the right indicating "Caution: Steep grade, loose gravel." At Y, veer right to bench.

1.2 This bench overlooks Loonsfoot Landing and boat launch and at time of writing (August 2003), was fairly close to a service station. The trail does continue (another 2.7 miles until it meets the gravel Tri-County Corridor Trail) as evidenced by the signature arch you see in the near distance. However, due to the extreme proximity of an ATV trail running parallel to the walking path, we opted not to include the remainder of the Osaugie Trail in this book. The Osaugie eventually ends at Moccasin Mike Road where there is a park and picnic area (see Bear Creek Park, pg. 185). To complete this section of the trail, turn around here and retrace path to trailhead.

2.4 Trailhead.

 Foot Note:

There is so much to see and do in Superior. For more information contact the Superior-Douglas County Visitor Center at (800) 942-5313 or www.visitdouglascounty.com.

SAYS WHO?

Wisdom comes with age—and exercise!

Persons who improved their aerobic fitness had increased cognitive abilities as they aged compared to those who remained sedentary.

Psychological Science [30]

Pattison State Park • Off U.S. 2, 13 miles south of Superior

- **Watch the Black River cascade over volcanic rock, plummeting 165' to the gorge below and forming Big Manitou Falls—the highest in Wisconsin!**

- **Allow plenty of time for this self-guided interpretive trail with many interesting features (guide booklet available at park office).**

- **Beautiful view of Interfalls Lake and three distinct platforms that offer a variety of angles from which to observe the falls and river gorge.**

TRAILHEAD DIRECTIONS & PARKING:
From the Superior-Douglas County Visitor Center, head west on U.S. 2 for 1.7 miles. Turn left (south) on WI 35 (Tower Ave) and travel 13 miles. Watch for sign for Pattison State Park. Turn left to park office. Ample parking with designated RV and wheelchair accessible parking available.

TRAILHEAD FACILITIES & FEES:
Park office has small gift shop, flush toilet (wheelchair accessible), water and picnic area (see Pattison State Park Main Picnic Area, pg. 186), mini outdoor fitness course, horseshoe pits, basketball hoop and volleyball court. Nature Center/Shelter features cultural and natural history including artifacts from the copper mining industry, Native American heritage, logging camps and a variety of animal and waterfowl displays. Annual or day use state park permit is required and available at park office.

TOTAL TRAIL LENGTH, SURFACE & WIDTH:
2.2 miles; paved, hardpacked dirt and gravel; average 5' wide. Minimal rock and root.

INCLINES & ALERTS:
There are three inclines ranging from 13–16°. Steepest incline is 16° for 20' at 1.8 miles on the return. No climbing in gorge area. Uneven pavement in areas.

CONTACT:
Pattison State Park: (715) 399-3111

MILEAGE & DESCRIPTION

0.0   Trailhead begins at sign indicating Big Manitou Falls. Your journey will begin through the picnic area. In just a short distance find Nature Center/Shelter. The exhibits found here provide insight into the unique history of Pattison State Park, its wildlife and geology. Turn right at trail intersection just beyond pay phone. Continue on paved path while enjoying the views of Interfalls Lake as you circle the picnic area.

At next trail intersection, veer left following sign to Big Manitou Falls.

0.1 Uneven and cracked pavement in this area—use caution. Several benches near Interfalls Lake provide a leisurely stop. Beach combers frequent the sandy lakeshore on warm days.

Soon you will see steps leading down to a stone circular area, which is the tunnel that goes under WI 35. You will return to this location, but first continue on paved path toward chain link fence and viewing area for dam and Interfalls Lake.

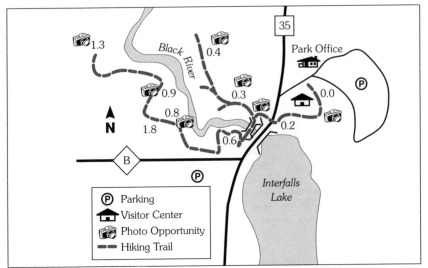

0.2 Return to previous stone circular area and descend 5 steps (cement, handrail), then 8 steps (cement, no handrail) leading to the tunnel. This 6'-tall, 6'-wide tunnel travels 60' under WI 35. At trail intersection, turn right. Nice views of Black River appear as it meanders its way toward the 165' plummet of Big Manitou Falls.

Continue to right and up 21 steps (wood and asphalt, no handrail) beside chain link fence. At intersection to right is a circular path that leads to a geological history sign, memorial marker and drinking fountain (seasonal).

0.3 Intersection to left leads to first overlook and Marker #1. Descend 25 steps (wood and asphalt, no handrail) to overlook (guardrail) with spectacular close-up view of the top of Big Manitou Falls. To the right see tree-covered river gorge. The dark brown rock in this area is basalt or trap rock, which is the solid remnant of ancient lava flows. The small pits marking the upper surface were formed by gas bubbles during the cooling process. Some of the larger pits previously held agates that have since been battered loose and washed up on Lake Superior's shores. Return to path.

Veer left at intersection to second overlook and Marker #2. Beyond cement platform descend 7 steps (cement, double handrail) to a wooden platform (guardrails) with full-length view of falls. Depending upon water flow, ribbons of water may offer a delicate touch to the thunderous roar of the falls.

Wooden benches provide a place to relax while viewing this majestic waterfall, river gorge and valley below. Guide booklet explains about the Douglas Fault, which extends from east of Ashland to the vicinity of the Twin Cities of Minnesota. Return to path.

Continue to left; descend 37 steps (wood and asphalt, non-continuous, no handrail). Surface changes to gravel and leads to stunning view of gorge and the Black River. Marker #3 can be found at the chain link fence. Portions of the park were the ancient beach of glacial Lake Duluth 10,000 years ago.

0.4 After enjoying this view, return up the same path. Ascend 37 steps (wood and asphalt, no handrail, non-continuous), pass the previous viewing areas, then descend 21 steps (wood and asphalt, no handrail).

0.5 Stay on paved path to right along river until you see the quaint wooden bridge crossing river. Notice bench to right neatly tucked beneath cedars, which provides a lovely view of the river and arched wooden bridge. Photo ops abound on both sides of this charming arched bridge (wood, double handrail). Cross river, then turn right at foot of bridge and stay on path closest to river.

0.6 Keep to right on path along fence for best views of river gorge. There are three small steps at the end of this short section (path visible on left can be used to avoid steps). Again, keep to right for best views.

As path turns away from river you will come upon two steps on left that go up to Marker #4. The pit seen here was made by copper miners over 100 years ago. This dig may show some of the bore holes used to blast the rock leaving a raw-faced, shallow pit with piles of fragments.

Continue straight until to you see sign to Big Manitou Falls parking lot, then turn right and continue along gravel shoulder of road. Do NOT cross road to next overlook area at this location.

0.7 At pedestrian crossing sign, turn right following paved path to Big Manitou Falls south vistas. Stay on path to right for shortest path to overlook. Path to left is wheelchair accessible and also leads to vault toilets and picnic area. Shorter path on right has a 30' section of decline at bottom just prior to overlook.

0.8 This overlook has the most spectacular viewing area of the falls. Rock barriers and a wooden bench are provided for your protection and comfort. This area also includes Marker #5. The melting of the glaciers carved out the gorge and shaped the beautiful waterfalls. Look for a triangular opening toward the left at base of falls. It is an old, abandoned copper mine.

Continue left to end of stone wall. Trail continues on a 4'-wide, paved path down to riverbed. Alert: This portion of trail has uneven sections of pavement and also contains a segment of steep decline (16° for 20'), which will be an incline on your return. Shortly you will come to a vista (guardrail) with a partial view of the falls (better view when leaves fall in autumn).

0.9 Marker #6 can be found at this stone overlook. The Black River has been carving this gorge since the retreat of the glaciers. The river was originally named Mucudewa Sebee, which means Black or Dark River, by the Ojibwa Indians. Pavement ends here and path changes to gravel, dirt, rock and sand. Soon you will cross a short bridge (wood, double handrail).

1.0 Cross another short bridge (wood, double handrail).

1.1 Enter a lovely stand of balsam fir, round a curve and see the first bench of this wooded section of the trail; it offers rest and a fine forest view.

1.2 Soon you will come to the longest section of decline followed by a large step down (12"). Descend a series of 4 steps (wood and root, no handrail, non-continuous). In 200' descend 24 steps (wood, double handrail) leading to the last stretch of trail and edge of the Black River.

1.3 At trail's end is the bottom of the gorge. Here you will find a wooden bench to view the Black River and sandstone wall. This also includes Marker #7 (Marker #8 can be found on Little Falls Hiking Trail pg. 54). The formation of this sandstone and layered sedimentary rock is similar to the Lake Superior shoreline on the Bayfield peninsula and Apostle Islands.

When you're ready, turn around and retrace path to trailhead. This initial section on the return seems steep because it is a sustained climb out of the wooded area.

1.8 Area of steepest incline (16° for 20').

2.2 Trailhead.

SAYS WHO?

Want to lose a few pounds or more? Get out-of-doors!

Walking 45–60 minutes a day was shown to improve fitness and reduce weight without dieting in overweight men.

Exercise and Sports Science Reviews [2]

Pattison State Park • Off U.S. 2, 13 miles south of Superior

- **Interfalls Lake provides a peaceful, tranquil respite.**
- **Striking views reflect the rumbling activity of the Black River.**

TRAILHEAD DIRECTIONS & PARKING:
From the Superior-Douglas County Visitor Center, head west on U.S. 2 for 1.7 miles. Turn left (south) on WI 35 (Tower Ave) and travel 13 miles. Watch for sign for Pattison State Park. Turn left to park office. Ample parking with designated RV and wheelchair accessible parking available.

TRAILHEAD FACILITIES & FEES:
Park office has small gift shop, flush toilet (wheelchair accessible), water and picnic area (see Pattison State Park Main Picnic Area pg. 186). Annual or day use state park permit is required and available at park office.

TOTAL TRAIL LENGTH, SURFACE & WIDTH:
2.0 miles; paved first 0.3 mile, average 6–8' wide; hardpacked dirt and gravel, average 1–3' wide. Minimal rock and root.

INCLINES & ALERTS:
There are no inclines greater than 10°. Trail narrows at several places with one steep dropoff. Possible washout area.

CONTACT:
Pattison State Park: (715) 399-3111

MILEAGE & DESCRIPTION

0.0 Trailhead begins at sign indicating Big Manitou Falls. After beginning your journey through the picnic area you will soon see a big stone building to the right. It is the Nature Center and definitely merits a visit as it houses interpretive displays of park history, wildlife and geology. Also noteworthy are the exhibits of mammals, birds, fish and rocks as well as the story of Pattison State Park. Turn left at trail intersection just beyond pay phone. Continue on paved path while enjoying the views of Interfalls Lake as you circle the picnic area.

0.1 At the Bath House, follow trail to the right toward Interfalls Lake. There is ample beach area for swimming (no lifeguard on duty) and many benches for relaxing. At trail intersection, turn right and follow sign for Beaver Slide Trail. Cross bridge (wood, no handrail).

0.2 Asphalt ends; trail changes to gravel and hardpacked dirt. At Y in trail turn right.

0.3 Short spur to the right leads to bench and nice view of lake. Take a moment to enjoy the tranquility found here. Beginning in this section, you will cross many short bridges (wood, no handrail). We mention them here but not throughout the remainder of the trail.

0.4 At trail intersection, turn right and follow sign to Beaver Slide Trail.

0.5 Descend 12 steps (wood, no handrail).

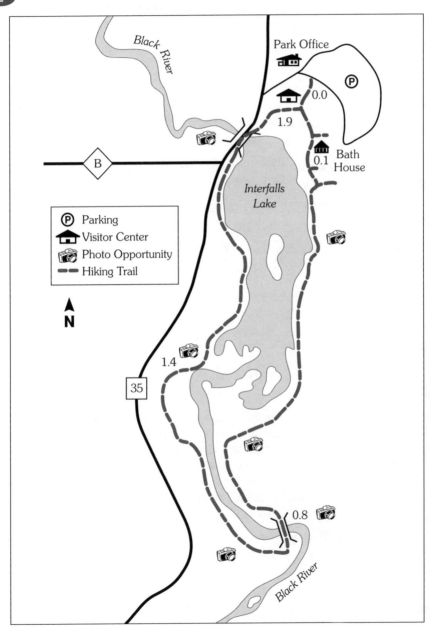

0.7 Listen carefully—in this section of the trail, the quietness of the lake acts as a foil to the rushing rapids of the Black River. When you arrive at the bench, enjoy the scenery. Observe the large white pines in this area.

0.8 Ascend 4 steps (cement, no handrail); cross bridge (wood, double handrails). The views of the river from this bridge are fabulous! Descend 5 steps (cement, no handrail). At trail intersection, turn right and a bench will be waiting for you on the left, offering more wonderful views of the Black River.

1.0 In this section, trail narrows at several places with one steep dropoff. Possible washout area.

1.1 Another bench for your river-viewing pleasure. Ascend 13 steps (wood, no handrail).

1.2 Ascend 30 steps (wood, no handrail). In approximately 200', descend first 11 steps (stone, no handrail), then 17 steps (wood, no handrail).

1.3 Descend 5 steps (wood, no handrail).

1.4 Ascend 6 steps (wood, no handrail). Bench with lovely river view. Descend 14 steps (wood, no handrail).

1.5 Ascend 11 steps (wood, no handrail).

1.6 Ascend 15 steps (wood, no handrail).

1.8 Trail opens in a grassy area that parallels WI 35. Continue straight toward bridge and across dam. This is one of the few places where you can actually stand above a dam and find some unique photo opportunities. Also, this platform offers one of the nicest unobstructed views of Interfalls Lake. This lake was constructed by the CCC and the island you see in the distance is manmade. Trail resumes on asphalt path near beach area, which has many benches.

1.9 Return to Nature Center. Water fountain on right. At intersection, turn left and retrace path to trailhead.

2.0 Trailhead.

Bench along the Beaver Slide Nature Trail. Photo by Melanie Morgan

DOG TRAIL

Pattison State Park • Off U.S. 2, 13 miles south of Superior

- **Beautiful wooded hike through the forest at Pattison State Park.**
- **The only trail specifically designated for your furry, four-legged friend.**

TRAILHEAD DIRECTIONS & PARKING:

From the Superior-Douglas County Visitor Center, head west on U.S. 2 for 1.7 miles. Turn left (south) on WI 35 (Tower Ave) and travel 13 miles. Watch for sign for Pattison State Park. Turn left to park office. Trailhead parking is 0.5 mile from park office. Drive straight ahead and turn right at stop sign. Follow arrows to campground entrance. Drive toward camp site #7 but turn right into Ski Trail parking area (paved).

TRAILHEAD FACILITIES & FEES:

Park office has small gift shop, flush toilet (wheelchair accessible), water and picnic area (see Pattison State Park Main Picnic Area pg. 186). Annual or day use state park permit is required and available at park office.

TOTAL TRAIL LENGTH, SURFACE & WIDTH:

1.4 miles; grass, hardpacked dirt and gravel; average 6–8' wide. Minimal rock and root.

INCLINES & ALERTS:

There are no inclines greater than 10°. Trailhead may be difficult to locate. Trail may have standing water in sections. Drive to trailhead requires traveling through campground; please use caution and watch for pedestrians.

CONTACT:

Pattison State Park: (715) 399-3111

MILEAGE & DESCRIPTION

0.0   To locate trailhead from parking area, DO NOT head toward No Bicycle symbol. Instead turn around and head southeast toward Service Road sign, continuing to Pet symbol. Trailhead begins here on 8'-wide gravel path.

0.2   Spur to right is part of North Country National Scenic Trail system that runs through Pattison State Park. For more information regarding this National Trail that spans seven states, see Foot Note from Three Bridges Trail (pg. 94). Stay on main path and continue straight. In 400' cross boardwalk.

0.3   Cross bridge (wood, double handrail) over small creek.

0.4   Cross another section of boardwalk.

0.5   Find a bench that provides a lovely view of the Black River. The bridge you see is part of the Beaver Slide Nature Trail (pg. 48).

0.6   Spur to right; continue on main trail.

0.7 Ski Trail sign at trail intersection. Here the trail branches in two directions. To the right, the ski trail continues, but exceeds *Gentle Hikes* trail length limit. To the left, the ski trail continues through a wet, high grass area leading to park road. Our advice at this juncture is to turn around and retrace path to trailhead and enjoy this splendid wooded hike again en route to its beginning.

1.4 Trailhead.

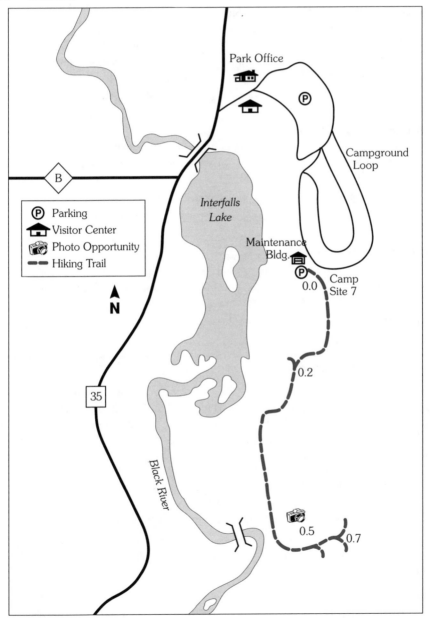

 **LITTLE FALLS HIKING TRAIL**

Pattison State Park • Off U.S. 2, 14 miles south of Superior

- **Lovely views of Little Manitou Falls.**
- **Hike in proximity to the scenic Black River.**

TRAILHEAD DIRECTIONS & PARKING:
From the Superior-Douglas County Visitor Center, head west on U.S. 2 for 1.7 miles. Turn left (south) on WI 35 (Tower Ave) and travel 13 miles. Watch for sign for Pattison State Park. Continue on WI 35 for 1 additional mile south of main entrance to Pattison State Park. Follow sign and turn left to paved parking areas. Lower lot has designated RV and wheelchair accessible parking. Upper lot for overflow parking or access to canoe pullout.

TRAILHEAD FACILITIES & FEES:
Vault toilets, water and picnic area nearby (see Little Manitou Falls Picnic Area pg. 187). Annual or day use state park permit is required and available at park office.

TOTAL TRAIL LENGTH, SURFACE & WIDTH:
1.3 miles; paved, gravel, hardpacked dirt; average 3' wide. Minimal rock and root.

INCLINES & ALERTS:
There are two inclines ranging from 12–20°. Steepest incline is 20° for 10' at 1.2 miles. You will need to cross entrance road to locate trailhead. Uneven asphalt. Trail comes close to river at several points.

CONTACT:
Pattison State Park: (715) 399-3111

MILEAGE & DESCRIPTION

0.0 Trailhead begins across the entrance road from the parking area. Enter on
 asphalt surface and descend 7 steps (wood, handrail). Immediately you will hear the sounds of Little Manitou Falls as it comes into view. The 31' falls are part of the Black River, which actually begins its journey 22 miles southwest of Pattison State Park at Black Lake on the Wisconsin-Minnesota border (for more information pick up the Pattison State Park Visitor—a free newspaper available at park office). There is a bench to the left for spectacular falls viewing. As you continue, an even better view of the falls becomes apparent. Little Manitou Falls is very picturesque regardless of water flow levels so bring the camera.

0.2 This section contains 4 bridges (wood, no handrail) and one bench that offers
 lovely river views.

0.4 At trail intersection, turn left and cross bridge (spur to right leads to river's
 edge). Ascend 5 steps (wood, no handrail).

0.5 Continue to follow main trail (spur to right leads to river's edge). In approximately 1000', trail intersects with Beaver Slide Nature Trail (see pg. 48). This bridge affords beautiful views up- and downriver. A bench allows you to rest a while and enjoy these natural surroundings. Turn around here and retrace path to trailhead.

1.2 Area of steepest incline (20° for 10').

1.3 Trailhead.

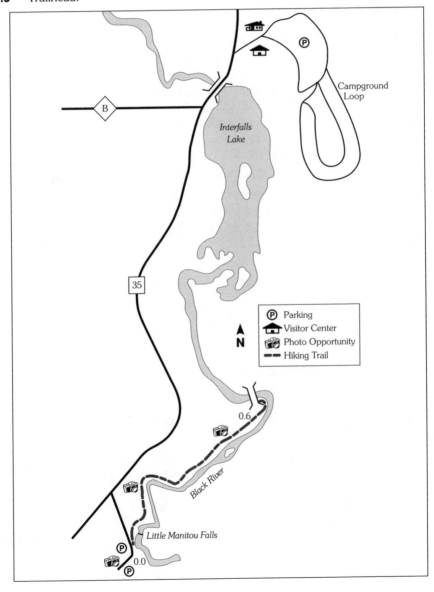

Interfalls Lake

Campground Loop

B

35

℗	Parking
🏠	Visitor Center
📷	Photo Opportunity
▬▬	Hiking Trail

N

0.6

Black River

Little Manitou Falls

0.0

Amnicon Falls State Park • Off U.S. 2, 12 miles from Superior, 87 miles from Hurley

- **Allow plenty of time for this self-guided, interpretive trail with many interesting features (guide booklet available at park office).**

- **This trail showcases four wonderful falls including the spectacular Upper and Lower Falls of the Amnicon River.**

- **Historically significant bowstring bridge over the Amnicon River above Lower Falls.**

TRAILHEAD DIRECTIONS & PARKING:

On U.S. 2, turn north on County Road U for 0.3 mile; turn left at sign for Amnicon Falls State Park. From office parking area, turn right following flow of river and drive 0.3 mile to large paved parking lot (designated wheelchair accessible parking) at end of drive. RV travelers: Please turn left at first stop sign, then take a right and travel over the bridge. Parking is available near open-sided shelter or at the next right in paved lot.

TRAILHEAD FACILITIES & FEES:

Vault toilets (wheelchair accessible), water, tables, grills. Annual or day use state park permit is required and available at park office.

TOTAL TRAIL LENGTH, SURFACE & WIDTH:

0.5 mile; hardpacked dirt, gravel. Width difficult to determine because of terrain change. Minimal rock and root.

INCLINES & ALERTS:

There are no inclines greater than 10°. Steep cliffs with no guardrails.

CONTACT:

Amnicon Falls State Park: (715) 398-3000

MILEAGE & DESCRIPTION

0.0 Although scenic and beautiful in its own right, this trail is best known for its

interpretive features. Please be sure to pick up a guide booklet from the park office. Some of the information presented below was found there. Only numbers are posted on interpretive signs throughout the trail, so a booklet explaining them is a necessity.

Trailhead begins at west corner of parking area on 6'-wide paved path by Douglas Fault informational kiosk. There are numerous benches throughout this trail. You can clearly see and hear Upper Amnicon Falls from this point. Do not cross bridge at this point; rather, turn left and walk along the pavement upriver. Ascend 5 gradual steps (wood and pavement, no handrail), which bring you to a park informational kiosk as well as a spectacular view of Upper Amnicon Falls and Marker #1.

Marker #1 is the first interpretive marker of this Geology Walk. From this point, retrace steps back to covered bridge; do not cross bridge but continue down 7 steps (wood and hardpack dirt, no handrail) and up 1 step to Marker #2. It is in this area you will find picturesque views of Lower Falls and sandstone. Alert: Steep cliffs with no guardrail—use caution.

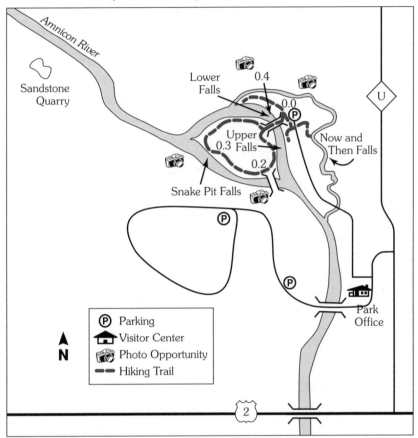

0.1 Return to covered bridge and cross. This is one of only six bowstring bridges in existence today designed by Charles Horton. He claimed that his design, absent of rivets and bolts, would allow for quick assembly without the added expense of machinery and tools. Read more in the park's visitor paper.

After crossing this historical bridge, the trail becomes loosely defined for the remainder of hike. Meander left to Marker #3 and enjoy a different view of Upper Falls while also viewing the outstanding geologic feature of the park—the Douglas Fault. This Fault extends from Ashland to the Twin Cities of Minnesota! Alert: Steep cliffs with no guardrail. Continue along path up small incline and ascend 9 steps (wood and dirt, no handrail) staying toward the left following trail upstream.

0.2 Marker #4 is located at a small stone bridge where the river separates. Look to the opposite river bank to find a rock that was brought here by the glaciers—granite gneiss studded with red garnet crystals.

Do not cross bridge, but continue to the right along the west branch of the river downstream to Marker #5. Note the different colors within the basalt and look for small pits on the upper surface of rocks—the larger were the original "homes" of the famous Lake Superior agates!

This is an incredibly scenic section of the trail with gorgeous cascades of rushing rapids on one side and a towering stand of pine on the other. At Marker #6 enjoy Snake Pit Falls—magnificent in high water conditions. Alert: Steep cliff with no guardrail.

0.3 Continue to follow curve of island toward Marker #7, which sports another rock type: breccia.

0.4 This section of trail brings you back to the covered bridge. Cross it, turn right and ascend 5 gradual steps (wood and pavement, no handrail), which bring you to Marker #8. If water is low, look at the downstream edge of the deep plunge pool beneath the falls to see nearly vertical sandstone beds created by fault action.

Descend 19 uneven steps (rock, handrail) to observation deck for fantastic close-up view of Upper Falls. It is not often that a trail offers such proximity to so much power! Spend some time here soaking in this sight. When ready, ascend steps and continue straight on pavement, crossing the entrance road to Marker #9 for Now and Then Falls. Depending on water conditions, this may or may not be flowing (hence the name), but if it is, have your camera handy as it is very picturesque. Retrace path to trailhead.

0.5 Parking lot and trailhead.

Foot Note:

Want to get more involved in helping Amnicon Falls or Pattison State Parks?

Consider joining the Friends group by writing to Amnicon and Pattison State Parks, 6294 S. State Rd. 35, Superior, WI 54880

Bowstring Bridge and Lower Falls. Photo by Ladona Tornabene

AMNICON FALLS PICNIC STROLL*

Amnicon Falls State Park • Off U.S. 2, 12 miles from Superior, 87 miles from Hurley • *Gentle Hikes name

- **Majestic views of Upper Amnicon Falls and continuous views of Amnicon River for first 0.3 mile of trail.**

- **Historically significant bowstring bridge over the Amnicon River above the Lower Falls.**

TRAILHEAD DIRECTIONS & PARKING:

On U.S. 2, turn north on County Road U for 0.3 mile; turn left at sign for Amnicon Falls State Park. From office parking area, turn right following flow of river and drive 0.3 mile to large paved parking lot (designated wheelchair accessible parking) at end of drive. RV travelers: Please turn left at first stop sign, then take a right and travel over the bridge. Parking is available near open-sided shelter or at the next right in paved lot.

TRAILHEAD FACILITIES & FEES:

Vault toilets (wheelchair accessible), water, tables, grills. Annual or day use state park permit is required and available at park office.

TOTAL TRAIL LENGTH, SURFACE & WIDTH:

0.6 mile; hardpacked dirt, gravel, grass. Width varies and was difficult to determine because of terrain change. Minimal rock and root.

INCLINES & ALERTS:

There are no inclines greater than 10°. Use caution—portions of the trail are on park roads.

CONTACT:

Amnicon Falls State Park: (715) 398-3000

MILEAGE & DESCRIPTION

0.0   Trailhead begins at west corner of parking area on 6'-wide paved path by
 Douglas Fault informational kiosk. There are numerous benches throughout
 this trail. You can clearly see and hear Upper Amnicon Falls from this point. However, instead of crossing bridge, turn left and walk along the pavement up river. Ascend 5 gradual steps (wood and pavement, no handrail), which bring you to a park informational kiosk as well as a spectacular view of Upper Amnicon Falls! By now you may have noticed Markers #1 and #8; this section of the trail is also part of the Amnicon Falls Geology Walk (see pg. 56). Pavement ends; loosely defined trail continues along river's edge upstream.

0.1   This section of the trail takes you along and on the park road, which is shared with vehicles—use caution. As you approach a concrete embankment, be careful as there is no guardrail.

0.2   In this section, the trail is shared with a one-lane bridge and vehicles. In approximately 200', trail meanders off road again.

0.3 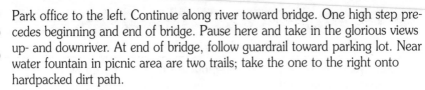 Park office to the left. Continue along river toward bridge. One high step precedes beginning and end of bridge. Pause here and take in the glorious views up- and downriver. At end of bridge, follow guardrail toward parking lot. Near water fountain in picnic area are two trails; take the one to the right onto hardpacked dirt path.

0.4 At trail intersection, turn left. Shortly you will notice another water fountain; at next intersection, turn right. The bench here provides river views. You will arrive at another picnic area with a separate parking lot that is wheelchair accessible (see Amnicon Falls State Park Accessible Picnic Area pg. 188). Continue on trail.

0.5 Cross bridge (wood, double handrail); descend 5 uneven steps (stone, double wall). Alert: Pavement uneven at base of steps. River splits beneath the bridge creating a highly scenic location. At trail intersection, turn right and continue along the main branch of river. Shortly, descend 9 steps (wood and gravel, no handrail). Continue through a marvelous forest of towering pines toward covered bowstring bridge.

0.6 Cross covered bowstring bridge, which provides wonderful views of Upper Amnicon Falls. This is one of only six bowstring bridges in existence today designed by Charles Horton. He claimed that his design, absent of rivets and bolts, would allow for quick assembly without the added expense of machinery and tools. Read more about this in the park's visitor paper. This returns you to trailhead and parking area.

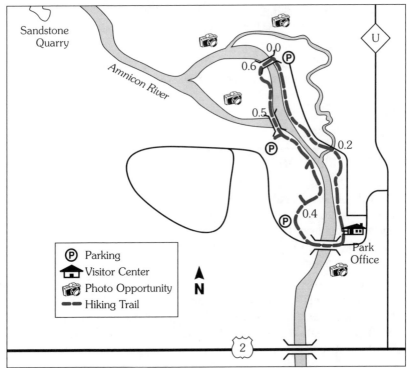

THIMBLEBERRY NATURE TRAIL

Amnicon Falls State Park • Off U.S. 2, 12 miles from Superior, 87 miles from Hurley

- **Allow plenty of time for this self-guided interpretive trail with many diverse features (guide booklet available at park office).**

- **Interesting views of Amnicon River from several overlooks.**

- **Trail opens at the halfway point to reveal lovely meadow sporting a variety of wildflowers in summer months.**

- **Our cover photo was shot on this hike.**

TRAILHEAD DIRECTIONS & PARKING:
On U.S. 2, turn north on County Road U for 0.3 mile; turn left at sign for Amnicon Falls State Park. From office parking area turn left at stop sign, then right and over bridge following signs for Campground and Nature Trail. Drive 0.3 mile to small gravel parking area on left across road from Nature Trail. RV parking is available near open-sided shelter or second paved lot en route to Nature Trail parking.

TRAILHEAD FACILITIES & FEES:
Water. Annual or day use state park permit is required and available at park office.

TOTAL TRAIL LENGTH, SURFACE & WIDTH:
1.0 mile; hardpacked dirt, gravel, grass. Width varies from 1–6'. Minimal rock, moderate root, heavy in sections.

INCLINES & ALERTS:
There are no inclines greater than 10°. Must cross park road to access trailhead. No pets or bikes allowed on trail. Overgrowth may be problematic in summer.

CONTACT:
Amnicon Falls State Park: (715) 398-3000

MILEAGE & DESCRIPTION

0.0 Trailhead begins across road from parking area on gravel path at sign indicating Thimbleberry Nature Trail. Although scenic and beautiful in its own right, this trail is best known for its interpretive features, so make sure to pick up a guide booklet from the park office. Some of the information presented below was found there. Only numbers are posted on interpretive signs throughout the trail, so a booklet explaining them is a necessity.

Shortly you will encounter the trail intersection; veer right on main trail and descend 22 steps (wood and gravel, no handrail, non-continuous), then continue down 5 additional steps (wood and gravel, no handrail, non-continuous). Soon you will arrive at Marker #1 "Tree of Life." Guide booklet explains how it got this name.

Descend 3 steps (wood and gravel, no handrail, non-continuous) to bridge (wood, double handrail) and Marker #2 "A Tart Treat." A taste to try and love, but only if there are more than ten berries on the shrub!

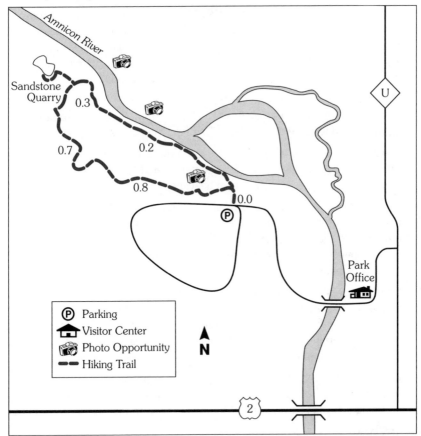

0.1 You will come to the first overlook, which yields a partial view of the Amnicon River; however, better views await some 200' further on trail at second overlook. In this section you will encounter areas of moderate to heavy root.

0.2 The third overlook provides a lovely view of Amnicon River. Trail begins to follow closely along the river and brings you to Marker #3 "Rope Tree." Read your guide to find out how rope was made from tree bark.

In 300' ascend 18 steps (wood and gravel, handrail, non-continuous); however, before ascending, pause to take in magnificent river views and majestic stand of white and red pines!

0.3 Marker #4 "Where Fish Spawn." Amnicon literally means "where fish spawn." You can learn more about the Ojibwa lifestyle from the guide book.

In 200' find spur to Sandstone Quarry. This is an interesting feature of the trail and we recommend that you turn right and follow the spur trail. At Y, turn left and continue to small deck overlooking quarry lake where you will find a sign posted with information about the quarry. Stop here at this deck, then return to main trail. Please do not continue on path around Quarry due to serious erosion problems that pose a safety hazard.

0.5 Main trail continues to Marker #5 "Band-Aids and Glue." See the two common
 trees that played an integral role in Native American life and canoe maintenance. Shortly you will ascend 7 steps (wood and gravel, no handrail, non-continuous). The trail surface changes to grass before you enter a lovely open meadow. Wildflowers are found in abundance during summer months.

0.6 Marker #6 "A Wild Garden." Using your guide booklet, see how many plants you can identify. If you enjoy this activity, we strongly recommend that you bring along a wildflower guidebook (see Appendix A for suggestions).

In less than 200' you will enter through a dramatic canopy of fir and spruce (short section, but nice), which brings you to Marker #7 "Food, Fur Coats, and More." See the handicraft of a beaver.

0.7 Soon you will encounter a spur trail to a beaver dam. We recommend taking it to observe the marsh created as a result of the beaver's work. Return to the main trail to Marker #8 "A Winter Friend." See the tree that was used to make snowshoes. Later in this section there is a long gradual incline of 10° for approximately 300'.

0.8 Spur to service road; stay on main trail. Marker #9 "Children's Delight and Canoe Tree" may be easy to miss so look for it on the left side of trail approximately 80' from the spur to service road. Your booklet does a fine job of distinguishing between two trees whose identities are often confused—the aspen and the birch.

0.9 Cross bridge (wood, double handrail). Shortly, cross another bridge (wood, handrail). In this section is a spur to the campground. Please stay on main trail. At trail intersection, turn right to complete this loop and return to trailhead.

1.0 Trailhead.

Foot Note:

"In every walk with Nature one receives far more than he seeks."
John Muir, American Naturalist & Sierra Club founder.

Thimbleberry Nature Trail. Photo by Melanie Morgan

Brule River State Forest • Off U.S. 2, 28 miles from Superior, 72 miles from Hurley

- **Incredible wooded interpretive hike featuring a massive white pine measuring 11' in circumference!**

TRAILHEAD DIRECTIONS & PARKING:

From U.S. 2 in Brule, turn south on Anderson Road—the road immediately east of the Brule River Wayside. At sign for State Forest Campground do not turn right, but follow main road to sign for Nature Trail parking. Small paved parking area available by pole barn.

TRAILHEAD FACILITIES & FEES:

None. No fees for trail use.

TOTAL TRAIL LENGTH, SURFACE & WIDTH:

1.8 mile; hardpacked dirt; average 3–5' wide. Minimal rock and root.

INCLINES & ALERTS:

There are two inclines ranging from 14–18°. Steepest incline is 18° for 40' at 0.3 mile. No pets permitted on trail. Areas of washout and low-hanging branches possible.

Note: Changes in the interpretive signs are planned for implementation by the DNR in spring/summer 2004. Since exact locations of some signs have yet to be determined, the description herein reflects the current markers (July 2003) that will remain.

CONTACT:

Brule River State Forest: (715) 372-5678

MILEAGE & DESCRIPTION

0.0   Trailhead begins north of parking area on 5'-wide grassy path. Find sign indicating "Stony Hill Nature Trail." Immediately enter through a dramatic stand of pine as trail parallels the road. In approximately 300', look across the road for a glimpse of the beautiful Bois Brule campground. Shortly you will encounter another sign indicating "Stony Hill Nature Trail 1.6 mile loop," which marks a different entry point to the trail.

0.1   At Y, turn right (you will return on path to the left). Some washout in this area at time of writing (July 2003).

0.2   This is the site of the largest white pine on the trail (look to the right), which measures 11' in circumference!

0.3   Location of steepest incline (18° for 40').

0.7   At the peak of Stony Hill you will be standing 1181' above sea level. Placed near the remnants of the old fire tower are two benches that provide a nice respite. Here you'll find interesting information about Stony Hill. See if you can locate the Bennet Fire Tower about 10 miles to the southwest.

0.8   Enter Red Pine Lane. These pines were planted in 1916. Can you imagine what this trail may have looked like then? Approximately 400' further you will find an interpretive marker with an actual cross-section from a 50-year-old red pine. It tells quite a story. This location also gives info on how the Brule River State Forest is managed.

1.1   Trail is intersected by a service road; continue straight. In approximately 400' you will pass under a powerline.

1.7   At Y, spur to right goes to campground; continue on trail. When you reach the trail intersection mentioned at mile 0.1 above, turn right. You are back on the main trail again. At entry sign for Stony Hill Nature Trail, turn left and retrace path to trailhead.

1.8   Trailhead.

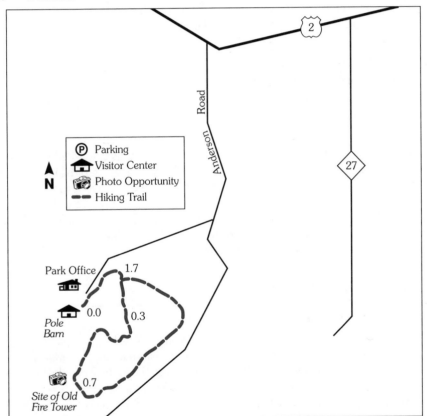

Foot Note:

Five of Wisconsin's top ten largest white pine are in the Brule Valley.
Source: Brule DNR

Brule River State Forest • Off U.S. 2, 28 miles from Superior, 72 miles from Hurley

- **Hike on the site of the first road connecting Superior and Bayfield, which was built in 1870.**

- **Trail features the old Percival Mine and the Clevedon Fire Tower.**

- **Walk through a striking, extraordinary area of northern hardwoods—the only one of its kind in the entire Brule River State Forest!**

TRAILHEAD DIRECTIONS & PARKING:

From U.S. 2 in Brule, turn north on County Road H and travel about 5 miles. At County Road FF turn left (west) and travel about 2 miles. At Clevedon Road turn left (south) on this gravel road. About 1.5 miles further you will come to a brown sign indicating Historical Bayfield Road Hiking Trail. Pull into the gravel lot.

TRAILHEAD FACILITIES & FEES:

None. No fees for trail use.

TOTAL TRAIL LENGTH, SURFACE & WIDTH:

2.5 miles; grass, boardwalk in sections; average 4' wide (contingent on mowing). Moderate rock, minimal root.

INCLINES & ALERTS:

There are four inclines ranging from 14–22°. Steepest incline is 22° for 7' at mile 1.0. Expect overgrowth during summer months. At time of hiking (August 2003), several sections of boardwalk were completely covered by long grass—use caution as the surface may be hidden. Stay outside the fence at Percival Mine site for your safety. DO NOT attempt to climb fire tower—it is illegal and unsafe. Areas of washout and low-hanging branches possible. Rocks in some areas may be loose. No bicycles or ATVs on trail.

CONTACT:

Brule River State Forest: (715) 372-5678

MILEAGE & DESCRIPTION

0.0 Trailhead begins at east corner of parking area on 4'-wide grassy path at map kiosk where a very informative one-page guide with map may be available. More information about this historical site is posted near trailhead. In 120' a trail intersection from the left is the return loop. Stay to the right; we thought some rocky sections were easier to ascend than descend. Soon sections of boardwalk begin; at time of writing some were severely overgrown—use caution.

0.4 Spur to left leads to old Percival Mine, which is marked by a fenced-in area. Path to this site is a rocky incline—use caution as some rock may be loose. For your safety, stay outside of fenced area.

0.6 As you approach a small bridge (wood, no handrail), a decline of 22° for 12' offers a steep and possibly slippery descent. Watch your footing and stay to the left because the decline is steepest to the right.

1.0 Some loose rock may be present on incline; trail begins to leave route previously used by the Bayfield Road in the 1800s. Shortly you will encounter the area of steepest incline (22° for 7') on the trail, then another incline (14° for 10') as the trail surface becomes more uneven.

1.3 The area of longest incline (14° for 95') is in this section. Pause often throughout this area and look around you. You will be treated to a spectacular 360° view of northern hardwoods. This the only area of its kind in the Brule River State Forest! Photo worthy.

1.5 The spur trail to the right leads to the Clevedon Fire Tower. It's worth the short jaunt to see it, but remember: do not climb the ladder. It is illegal and unsafe.

1.8 Back on the trail, notice the lovely cluster of basswood to the right. You will continue through the forest of hardwoods and conifers until you complete the loop and rejoin the beginning of the trail in about 0.7 mile.

2.5 When you reach the trail intersection, you will have come full circle; turn right and retrace trail for 130' to the parking area and trailhead.

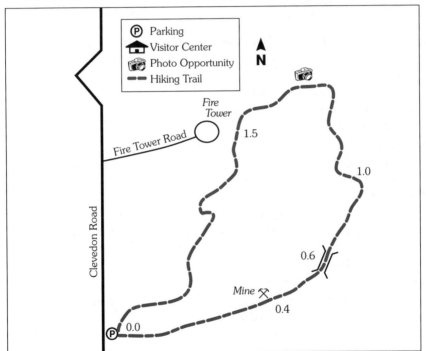

MARENGO RIVER TRAIL

North Country National Scenic Trail • Off U.S. 2, 55 miles from Superior, 45 miles from Hurley

- **Spectacular drive to this portion of the North Country National Scenic Trail.**
- **Sweeping vista of the Chequamegon-Nicolet National Forest.**

TRAILHEAD DIRECTIONS & PARKING:
From U.S. 2, turn south on U.S. 63 toward Grandview. Travel 13.6 miles to County Road D and turn south again. This drive is on the Wisconsin Color Tour for fall foliage. Locate brown sign for National Forest Campground and green sign for Lake Namekagon. Follow County Road D for 18.3 miles to Club Lake Road (gravel); turn left (east). Continue for 22.3 miles to Old Grade Road (at stop sign). Turn left (north); you should see a sign stating Color Tour #1. Travel on this road 24.3 miles to North Country Trail/Swedish Settlement marker; turn right into small gravel parking lot.

TRAILHEAD FACILITIES & FEES:
None. No fees for trail use.

TOTAL TRAIL LENGTH, SURFACE & WIDTH:
2.2 miles; hardpacked dirt; average 2' wide. Moderate rock and root.

INCLINES & ALERTS:
There is one incline of 16° for 35' at 1.3 miles on return. Wet areas and overgrowth may be problematic in summer. Some boards may be loose on bridge surface.

CONTACT:
Chequamegon-Nicolet National Forest (Glidden Office): (715) 264-2511

MILEAGE & DESCRIPTION

0.0 Trailhead begins at southeast corner of parking area on 1–2'-wide hardpacked dirt path. In 160' cross laid log path as you journey through a forest of spruce, balsam fir, aspen, ash, maple and basswood. Further along the trail cross bridge. Alert: Some boards may be loose.

0.6 Spur to right to overlook vista. If scrambling over rock was on your To Do List today, this earns a check-off. We thought the view was worth every step. Sweeping 180° vista from craggy outcrop over mostly deciduous Chequamegon-Nicolet National Forest. This may be phenomenal as a fall hike.

1.1 One step up to bridge (wood, double handrail). Views of the Marengo River abound in both directions. The trail does continue but exceeds the length parameters of this book. Turn around at this point and retrace path to trailhead.

1.3 Area of steepest incline (16° for 35').

2.2 Trailhead.

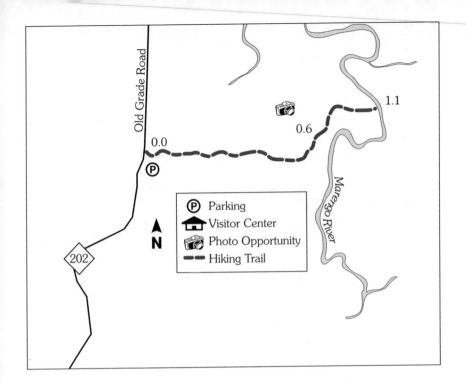

Do your energy levels need a spike? Take a hike!

Walking has been shown to result in a large increase in energy and vigor.

The Physician and Sports Medicine 2000 [25]

BOARDWALK TRAIL EAST LOOP

Northern Great Lakes Visitor Center • On U.S. 2, 60 miles from Superior, 40 miles from Hurley

- **Experience the variety of natural surroundings as you travel on a raised boardwalk through a wetland and sedge meadow.**
- **Observe the differences between a cold water spring-fed pond and a warm water pond.**
- **Good birding opportunities as trail leads into Whittlesey Creek National Wildlife Refuge.**

TRAILHEAD DIRECTIONS & PARKING:
From U.S. 2, turn west at County Road G and sign for Northern Great Lakes Visitor Center. Turn right into paved lot. Ample parking with designated RV and wheelchair accessible parking available.

TRAILHEAD FACILITIES & FEES:
Flush toilets (wheelchair accessible), water, gift shop, 9-county historical archives research center, educational programs, outstanding state-of-the-art exhibit hall, Intriguing Objects Theatre and interactive exhibits. No fees for use.

TOTAL TRAIL LENGTH, SURFACE & WIDTH:
0.5 mile; paved, gravel, boardwalk; average 5–6' wide.

INCLINES & ALERTS:
There are no inclines greater than 10°. The Visitor Center states that this trail meets Universal Design Standards (see pg. 208 for additional information). Due to sensitive vegetation, please stay on trail.

CONTACT:
Northern Great Lakes Visitor Center: (715) 685-9983

MILEAGE & DESCRIPTION

0.0 The best way to access the trailhead is to walk through the Visitor Center to
 the back right section just past the Coastal Wetlands Discovery Center and aquariums to the Whittlesey Conference and Reading Room. Go through this conference room to the exit door that leads out of the Visitor Center. Begin on paved trail; veer left at intersection and continue past spring-fed trout pond. After crossing bridge, path changes to gravel. On this loop trail, traffic noise is less filtered due to more open spaces.

0.1 Several benches are placed throughout this trail. In approximately 200' you
 will enter a boardwalk area that leads to a sedge meadow viewing platform with informational signs. For example, one of the signs just before the end of this section of boardwalk tells about the effects of alders on coastal wetlands.

0.3 At trail intersection, turn left.

0.4 At trail intersection, turn left to return to the Visitor Center. This concludes the East Loop of the trail. Trail does continue straight ahead, however, and connects with the West loop of the Boardwalk Trail (see pg. 74)

0.5 Trailhead.

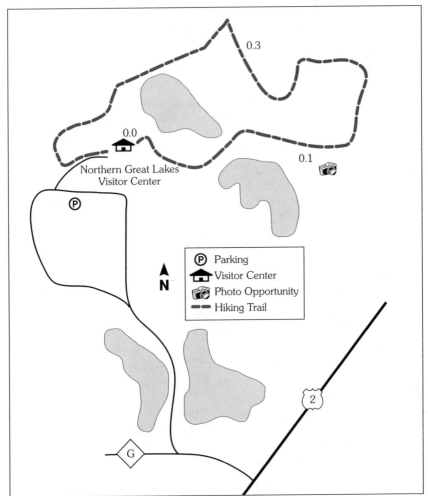

 SAYS WHO?

Got 5 minutes?

If you are currently inactive, walking for 5 minutes at a time, 6 times per day, on most days of the week can improve heart health.

Preventive Medicine [23]

BOARDWALK TRAIL WEST LOOP

Northern Great Lakes Visitor Center • On U.S. 2, 60 miles from Superior, 40 miles from Hurley

- **Experience the variety of natural surroundings as you travel on a raised boardwalk through a wetland and boreal forest.**
- **Portion of the trail showcases a dramatic wooded area of tamarack, cedar and spruce.**
- **Good birding opportunities.**

TRAILHEAD DIRECTIONS & PARKING:
From U.S. 2, turn west at County Road G and sign for Northern Great Lakes Visitor Center. Turn right into paved lot. Ample parking with designated RV and wheelchair accessible parking available.

TRAILHEAD FACILITIES & FEES:
Flush toilets (wheelchair accessible), water, gift shop, 9-county historical archives research center, educational programs, outstanding state-of-the-art exhibit hall, Intriguing Objects Theatre and interactive exhibits. No fees for use.

TOTAL TRAIL LENGTH, SURFACE & WIDTH:
0.5 mile; paved, gravel, boardwalk; average 5–6' wide.

INCLINES & ALERTS:
There are no inclines greater than 10°. The Visitor Center states that this trail meets Universal Design Standards (see pg. 208 for additional information). Due to sensitive vegetation, please stay on trail.

CONTACT:
Northern Great Lakes Visitor Center: (715) 685-9983

MILEAGE & DESCRIPTION

0.0 The best way to access the trailhead is to walk through the Visitor Center to the back, veering left toward the northwest door. Begin on paved trail; continue veering right on pavement past spring-fed pond to boardwalk. At the end of boardwalk, trail changes to gravel.

0.1 Benches are located at trail intersection; turn left. Boardwalk enters area over wetlands, then through an area of ash, alder and spruce. Benches are placed approximately 400' apart throughout this trail.

0.2 Here you will experience a dramatic change from wetlands to a dense boreal forest. Before locating the next bench you will return to the wetland area.

0.4 Find another bench before encountering the final stretch of boardwalk. At trail intersection, turn left and return to Visitor Center, which concludes the West Loop of the trail. (For Boardwalk Trail East Loop, see pg. 72.)

0.5 Trailhead.

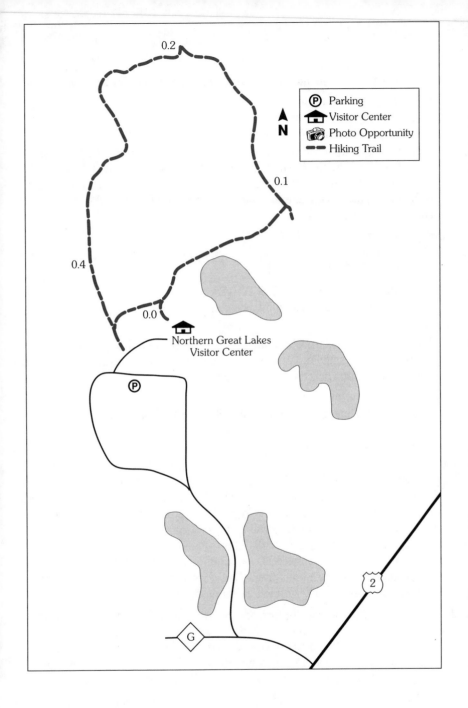

Northern Great Lakes
Visitor Center

ARTESIAN WAY

Prentice Park, Ashland • Off U.S. 2, 62 miles from Superior, 38 miles from Hurley

- **Several artesian wells and one crystal clear pool make this one a must see!**
- **Incredible wooded hike.**

TRAILHEAD DIRECTIONS & PARKING:
From U.S. 2 in the west end of Ashland, watch for large brown sign indicating City of Ashland Prentice Park. This can be found near Maslowski Beach. Turn south at sign on Turner Road and drive 0.2 mile to next sign. Turn right and continue to paved parking area near picnic pavilion. Designated RV and wheelchair accessible parking.

TRAILHEAD FACILITIES & FEES:
Flush toilets (wheelchair accessible), water, picnic area (see Prentice Park Picnic Area pg. 189). No fees for trail use.

TOTAL TRAIL LENGTH, SURFACE & WIDTH:
0.4 mile; paved, boardwalk, hardpacked dirt; average 2–3' wide.

INCLINES & ALERTS:
There are no inclines greater than 10°. Uneven section of boardwalk. Overgrowth and standing water may be problematic in summer. Galvanized steel drainage pipes on trails are slippery when wet.

CONTACT:
Ashland Area Chamber of Commerce: (800) 284-9484

MILEAGE & DESCRIPTION

0.0 Trailhead begins at park map kiosk near picnic pavilion on paved path. Continue toward lagoon. En route, notice artesian wells to the right of boardwalk. Just prior to lagoon, take boardwalk to right. To the left notice the blue WCC (Wisconsin Conservation Corps) 1990 sign posted at artesian pool overlooking the lagoon. Descend 3 steps (wood, double handrail) that indicates end of boardwalk. At intersection, continue straight. Take care on uneven section of boardwalk. Look for another artesian well bubbler. At next trail intersection, turn right (trail to left goes around a tree and to an older closed section of trail). Turn left at the next trail intersection.

0.1 See post with number 36; turn left. Spur trail to right leads to picnic area; continue straight. Cross bridge (wood, double handrail) over pool. Crystal clear waters beckon a closer look. Observe colorful rocks below surface and look for an intriguing underground artesian bubbler in sand. This may be a great spot for a picnic (note table nearby). Turn right at next trail intersection.

0.2 Follow path until you reach park entrance road. It appears trail may have previously continued to the left prior to the road; however, at time of writing (July 2003) it was impassable. Turn around and retrace path to trailhead.

0.4 Trailhead.

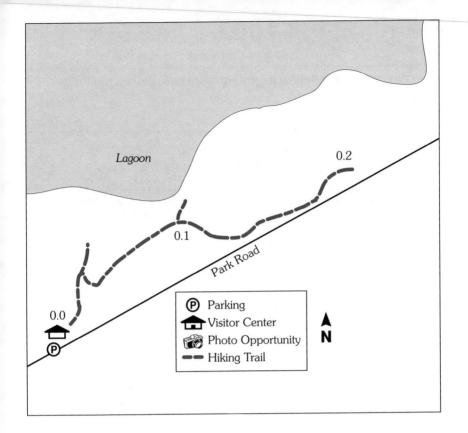

SAYS WHO?

Want to decrease your chances of having a stroke? Get in stride!

Walking briskly for about 30 minutes per day can reduce the risk of stroke by about 30%.

Journal of the American Medical Association [7]

CEDAR EDGE LOOP

Prentice Park, Ashland • Off U.S. 2, 62 miles from Superior, 38 miles from Hurley

- **See this natural habitat for migrating birds and nesting ground for mute swans.**
- **Picturesque views of lagoon.**

TRAILHEAD DIRECTIONS & PARKING:
From U.S. 2 in the west end of Ashland, watch for large brown sign indicating City of Ashland Prentice Park. This can be found near Maslowski Beach. Turn south at sign on Turner Road and drive 0.2 mile to next sign. Turn right and continue to paved parking area near picnic pavilion. Designated RV and wheelchair accessible parking.

TRAILHEAD FACILITIES & FEES:
Flush toilets (wheelchair accessible), water, picnic area (see Prentice Park Picnic Area pg. 189). No fees for trail use.

TOTAL TRAIL LENGTH, SURFACE & WIDTH:
0.3 mile; paved, boardwalk, gravel, hardpacked dirt; average 2–3' wide.

INCLINES & ALERTS:
There are no inclines greater than 10°; however, this is not a flat trail. Pavement uneven in places.

CONTACT:
Ashland Area Chamber of Commerce: (800) 284-9484

MILEAGE & DESCRIPTION

0.0 Trailhead begins at park map kiosk near picnic pavilion on paved path. There are several trail intersections off boardwalk, but continue straight toward lagoon. En route notice artesian wells to the right of boardwalk. You may choose to fill your water container here by taking the path off the boardwalk that leads to them. Continue straight toward lagoon. Go left along the boardwalk at lagoon. Look for various waterfowl including mute swans. This is a very picturesque spot. Plan to spend a little time here as this boardwalk offers 100' of wonderful lagoon-front scenery. Continue on boardwalk to the end where trail changes to gravel as it turns away from the lagoon and enters a lovely wooded area.

0.1 At trail intersection, turn right. Soon you will cross a brook that feeds into the lagoon. In 50' look left for unique sight—the northern cedar triplets!

0.2 Trail ends here at road. Turn around and retrace to trail intersection; turn right.

0.3 At next intersection, turn right and walk up hill past picnic area and steps to pavilion. Trailhead.

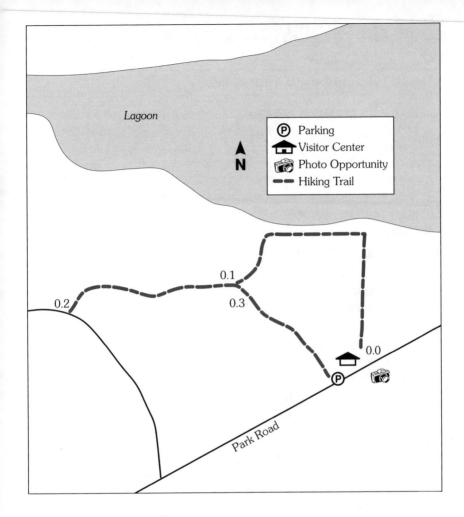

Lagoon

Parking
Visitor Center
Photo Opportunity
Hiking Trail

N

0.1

0.2

0.3

0.0

Park Road

 Foot Note:

At 100 acres, Prentice Park is the largest of Ashland's 12 parks.

 SAYS WHO?

Want to reduce your risk of getting cancer?

Physical activity such as walking may reduce the risk for colon cancer by as much as 50%.

Harvard Women's Health Watch [6,19]

MARSH VIEW WALK

Prentice Park, Ashland • Off U.S. 2, 62 miles from Superior, 38 miles from Hurley

- **Beautiful views of expansive marshland.**

TRAILHEAD DIRECTIONS & PARKING:

From U.S. 2 in the west end of Ashland, watch for large brown sign indicating City of Ashland Prentice Park. This can be found near Maslowski Beach. Turn south at sign on Turner Road and drive 0.2 mile to next sign. Turn right and continue past paved parking area. Turn again at first road to right. Follow map to lower gravel parking area. Limited space available.

TRAILHEAD FACILITIES & FEES:

No facilities available. No fees for trail use.

TOTAL TRAIL LENGTH, SURFACE & WIDTH:

0.2 mile; grass, gravel; average 8–10' wide.

INCLINES & ALERTS:

There are no inclines greater than 10°. Trail uneven in places.

CONTACT:

Ashland Area Chamber of Commerce: (800) 284-9484

MILEAGE & DESCRIPTION

 0.0 Trailhead begins from parking area at chain barricade and heads northwest toward marsh. In 400' ascend 8 steps (wood, double handrail) to a viewing platform with bench. Alert: Large step up, but we feel that the effort is worth the view as you look out over a highly scenic area of marshland. Notice the splendid field of cattails. This a beautiful expanse at any time but especially wonderful for viewing a sunset. Next to this observation deck is a bridge (wood, double handrail), which boasts another viewing area and affords a closer look at the lagoon. Watch for a variety of waterfowl as scenery abounds here.

0.1 We suggest that you stop at the end of this bridge and retrace path to trail-head. The trail does continue another 900' but takes on more traffic noise as it eventually ends abruptly at U.S. 2.

0.2 Trailhead.

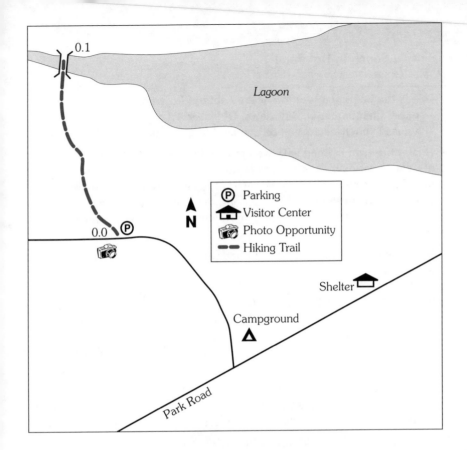

Maslowski Beach to Hot Pond
On U.S. 2, 62 miles from Superior, 38 miles from Hurley

- **This is the beginning section of the Ashland Bayfront Trail with unobstructed Chequamegon Bay views. Of historical significance is a Timeless Timber inscription on selected benches (see Foot Note below).**

- **This entire trail is lined with well-researched interpretive markers that are worth reading. This section features an overview of Ashland's history, ice cutting on the Bay, waterfront development, artesian well trivia, photos of the ship *Emerald* and the world's largest charcoal-fired iron blast furnace, "hot" fishing spots and Xcel Energy's contribution to this project.**

- **Near the end of this section is a good place to view freighters at the Reiss dock.**

TRAILHEAD DIRECTIONS & PARKING:
Located on U.S. 2, this is an easy location to find. Watch for brown sign indicating City of Ashland Maslowski Beach; turn in to paved parking. Ample space available in two lots; east lot has designated wheelchair accessible parking; west lot has paved access to the picnic shelter.

TRAILHEAD FACILITIES & FEES:
Flush toilets (wheelchair accessible), water, grills, playground, swimming beach, beach house, pay phone, bike rack. No fees for trail or picnic area usage.

TOTAL TRAIL LENGTH, SURFACE & WIDTH:
2.5 miles; paved; average 8' wide.

INCLINES & ALERTS:
There are no inclines greater than 10°. Must cross parking area 630' into trail. Trail passes very close to a major highway (U.S. 2). Highway reconstruction planned to begin by 2005. Although most of this trail is non-motorized, sections may be used by motorized vehicles accessing fishing area (see details in 0.7 mileage section below). Path may also be used by in-line skaters and cyclists. No lifeguard at beach area. Dogs much be leashed. Bring your own cleanup supplies; none provided.

CONTACT:
Ashland Area Chamber of Commerce: (800) 284-9484

MILEAGE & DESCRIPTION

0.0   Trailhead begins in the paved parking area that is furthest west near the first

interpretive marker, which is also furthest west. It can easily be missed so ensure that our description here matches what you see there. All official trail interpretive markers are nicely featured on rock face covered with acrylic. The interpretive marker of the trail provides information about Ashland's history, which we thought was a nice metaphor to combine trail beginnings with historical beginnings.

This section of trail parallels the sandy beach area that is home to various species of waterfowl. Sometimes the mute swan, which primarily dwells in the Prentice Park lagoon located nearby, makes its way into the Bay.

An interpretive marker here reveals how ice from Chequamegon Bay was harvested and stored for refrigeration until 1961. If Northland winters are not part of your routine, imagine what this spot might look like in January.

The picnic area to the left is described in further detail later in this book (see Maslowski Beach Picnic Area pg. 190).

This interpretive marker tells of the planning that went into the development of this trail, which involved Ashland's community as well as funding from a variety of agencies and businesses. This community takes pride in its bayfront.

Please note that you will find numerous benches throughout this entire trail. Most offer unobstructed bay views. Of historical significance is their Timeless Timber inscription (see Foot Note below).

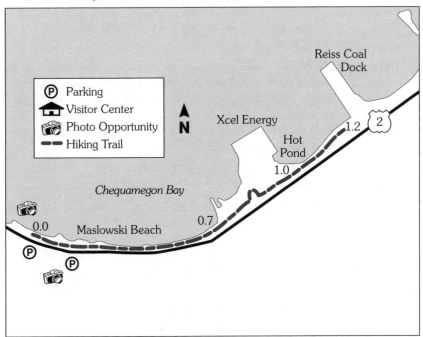

0.1   As you come to picnic tables located on a tiny peninsula with wonderfully scenic views, the trail becomes temporarily interrupted by the parking area. Use caution and common sense when crossing. Take time to read about the Radisson-Groseilliers cabin, which is located near the highway side of the parking area.

Further on in the parking area lies a busy spot—and busy for good reason.

Inside a partially enclosed wooden building is an artesian well that runs year-round. A good rule of thumb is to drink one cup of water for every 15 minutes of walking on the trail so let your cup run over here! Next to the well, find another interpretive marker, which explains why artesian wells have attracted people to this area for centuries.

0.3 Trail continues as it passes behind Bodin's on the Lake, which carries gifts, snacks, bicycles and other outdoor gear. As you walk along the Bayfront, note how the trees have been sculpted and shaped by the winds and weather of this region. Alert: For the next 0.4 mile, use caution as the trail comes very close to busy U.S. 2.

This interpretive marker features a photo of the ship, the *Emerald*. Here the story is told of that once familiar and historic vessel that was built in 1862, but now lies sunken in less than 15' of water not far from where you are standing.

0.7 Alert: As trail continues to parallel U.S. 2, there is an entrance drive from the highway on the right side that is not marked. Vehicles may be entering from U.S. 2 or exiting from the trail directly in front of you. At time of writing (June 2003), motor vehicles have access to fishing area near this location and are permitted to drive on the very section of paved trail you are about to enter. Use caution as there are no signs posted to alert trail users of this potential danger.

0.9 This interpretive marker shows a photo of the largest charcoal fired iron blast furnace in the world, built in Ashland in 1886 just south of Lake Superior. Although no longer standing, you can read about it here. Later this facility was used as a finishing plant for black granite—so valued that John F. Kennedy selected it for his gravestone when visiting Ashland in 1963, just two months prior to his assassination.

1.0 Sign indicating No Motorized Vehicles, Xcel Energy Plant. Stay on trail. In about 1000' you will reach the Hot Pond and public boat launch area.

1.2 As the Hot Pond and public boat launch area come into view, find another interpretive marker, which provides information regarding fish species found in this area of the Bay as well as why this pond does not freeze in winter. Xcel Energy supplied Ashland with this much-used park and boat ramp. This is also a good place to view freighters at the Reiss dock to the east.

We chose to end this section of the trail just prior to crossing Xcel's entrance road. You can see that the trail does continue (see Hot Pond to Reiss Coal Dock pg. 86). To complete this section, turn around and retrace path to trailhead.

2.4 Trailhead.

Foot Note:

Notice a Timeless Timber inscription on trail benches? The lumber used represents a portion of the only significant remaining supply of timber cut from the North American virgin forests (250-500 years old when cut). Recovered from freshwater lakes some 75-150 years later, it is now processed at the Timeless Timber facility in Ashland, which also houses a unique gift shop and video showcasing footage of the discovery! Call: (888) OLD-LOGS or www.timelesstimber.com.

 SAYS WHO?

Feeling stressed out? Get out and about!

Walking 30 minutes 4-6 days per week at a moderate pace can help to prevent or reduce stress and anxiety.

Exercising Your Way to Better Mental Health [44,42,43,27,25,26]

ASHLAND BAYFRONT TRAIL

Hot Pond to Reiss Coal Dock

On U.S. 2, 63 miles from Superior, 37 miles from Hurley

- **This entire trail is lined with well-researched interpretive signs that are worth reading. This section features an overview of the history of Ashland's electricity, industry and lumber mills.**

- **This section also takes on a more woodsy feel as trees buffer highway sights and sounds.**

TRAILHEAD DIRECTIONS & PARKING:

From U.S. 2, turn toward bay at 11th Avenue W on in-drive for Xcel Energy plant and follow for 0.1 mile to paved parking area. Ample space available.

TRAILHEAD FACILITIES & FEES:

Portable toilet, table, grill, boat launch, bike rack. No fees for usage.

TOTAL TRAIL LENGTH, SURFACE & WIDTH:

0.8 mile; paved; average 6–8' wide.

INCLINES & ALERTS:

There are no inclines greater than 10°. Path may also be used by in-line skaters and cyclists. Dogs much be leashed. Bring your own cleanup supplies; none provided.

CONTACT:

Ashland Area Chamber of Commerce: (800) 284-9484

MILEAGE & DESCRIPTION

0.0 Trailhead begins from north end of parking area on paved path.

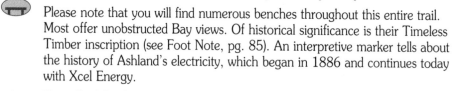 Please note that you will find numerous benches throughout this entire trail. Most offer unobstructed Bay views. Of historical significance is their Timeless Timber inscription (see Foot Note, pg. 85). An interpretive marker tells about the history of Ashland's electricity, which began in 1886 and continues today with Xcel Energy.

0.1 Reiss Coal Dock to the east is the only active commercial dock remaining in Chequamegon Bay. The interpretive marker reveals what industrial life was like for Ashland in the mid-1800s. This marker provides a vivid description of the site as it was back then.

0.3 Near this bench, look around the area for mill bolts, sawdust or slabs that have been washed ashore as they are remnants of the two huge lumber mills that occupied this site near the turn of the century. An interpretive marker provides history about the mills and log identification procedures that were used.

0.4 This section of the Ashland Bayfront Trail ends at 6th Avenue West. Retrace path to trailhead.

0.8 Trailhead.

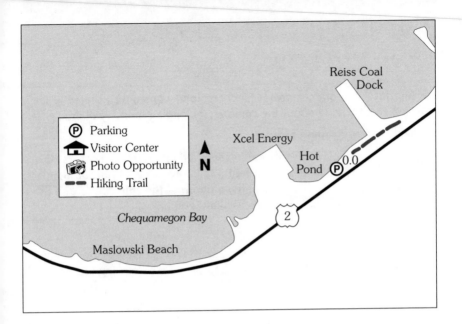

 SAYS WHO?

Joint pain keeping you off the trail?

Jarring forces on knees and other joints can be reduced by 12-25% by using hiking poles.

Harvard Women's Health Letter [49]

Memorial Park to Krehar Park

On U.S. 2, 64 miles from Superior, 36 miles from Hurley

- **Memorial Park commemorates local men and women who served in the Armed Forces. Read about the commercial logging industry of eras past.**
- **Lovely vista of Ashland Marina.**
- **This entire trail is lined with well-researched interpretive markers that are worth reading. This section features an overview of harbor history, Ashland's culturally diverse origins, a photo of the ship** *Stella* **and tales of her adventures, and the city's lumber companies.**

TRAILHEAD DIRECTIONS & PARKING:

Located on U.S. 2, this is an easy location to find just west of the park and the Chequamegon Hotel. Watch for turn-in to small paved parking area (accessible from east end only). Designated wheelchair accessible parking available.

TRAILHEAD FACILITIES & FEES:

No facilities at trailhead; however, there are facilities at Krehar Park (see Krehar Park to Water Plant pg. 90) at the end of this trail. No fees for usage.

TOTAL TRAIL LENGTH, SURFACE & WIDTH:

1.3 miles; paved; average 6–8' wide. Although paved, surface is uneven in places. Approximately 300' of trail is on old railroad bed at 0.2 mile.

INCLINES & ALERTS:

There is one incline of 12° for 25' at 0.9 mile on return. Must cross marina entrance road at 0.3 mile into trail. Path may also be used by in-line skaters and cyclists. Dogs much be leashed. Bring your own cleanup supplies; none provided.

CONTACT:

Ashland Area Chamber of Commerce: (800) 284-9484

MILEAGE & DESCRIPTION

0.0

Trailhead begins from west end of parking area at bench and interpretive marker that reveals the history of this fine harbor. Begin on 5'-wide boardwalk. Shortly you will encounter an observation deck with benches and a telescope for a closer look at lake activity. Soon the boardwalk ends and pavement begins.

Please note that you will find numerous benches throughout this entire trail. Most offer unobstructed Bay views. Of historical significance is their Timeless Timber inscription (see Foot Note, pg. 85).

0.1

Enter Memorial Park and read about the commercial logging industry of eras past. See cannon caisson and marker commemorating local men and women who served in the U.S. Armed Forces. Follow paved path to overlook of harbor. Continue on path behind bandshell to steps. Descend 11 steps (wood, double handrail, non-continuous). You will find a bench before descending 33 additional steps (wood, double handrail, non-continuous).

0.2 Find 3 benches before descending 9 steps (wood, double handrail, non-continuous) to railroad tracks. Turn right on tracks toward road.

0.3 Do not cross road at this point but turn left and follow pavement to boardwalk. At end of boardwalk, turn right and cross marina entrance road to pavement on other side—use caution. Turn left on pavement and pick up trail at bench. Continue right down slope, which will be the incline upon return. Alert: Uneven pavement. The interpretive marker in this section tells of Ashland's diverse origins.

0.4 Paved spur to right leads to quaint gazebo and picnic table. Continue on path over short section of boardwalk. A number of benches are available for your viewing pleasure. Shortly, an interpretive marker features a photo of the ship *Stella* and her interesting adventures!

0.6 The last interpretive marker of this section is about the lumber companies, their financial troubles at the turn of the century and how they overcame such struggles. The trail continues (see Krehar Park to Water Plant, pg. 90). To complete this section, turn around and retrace path to trailhead.

0.9 Location of steepest incline (12° for 25').

1.3 Trailhead.

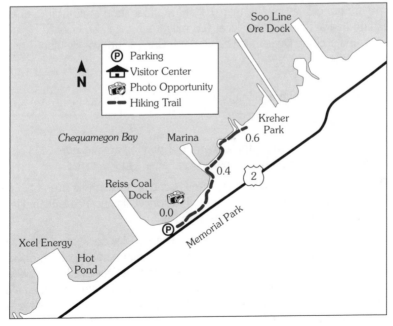

ASHLAND BAYFRONT TRAIL

Krehar Park to Water Plant
On U.S. 2, 64 miles from Superior, 36 miles from Hurley

- **This entire trail is lined with well-researched interpretive markers that are worth reading. This section features information about the world's largest dock (inactive), boat house history and historical Bay City River.**
- **Quaint boathouse area.**
- **Portions of this section of the trail offer a more remote feeling with many opportunities for bird watching.**

TRAILHEAD DIRECTIONS & PARKING:
From U.S. 2, turn northwest on Prentice Ave (between 3rd and 5th Avenues E) toward Chequamegon Bay and follow for 0.1 mile to park entrance. Ample paved parking available with designated wheelchair accessible and RV spaces.

TRAILHEAD FACILITIES & FEES:
Flush toilets (wheelchair accessible), water, grills, playground, swimming beach, fishing pier, boat launch, pay phone, RV designated campground (no tents). No fees for picnic area/trail usage, but $20 fee per day for campground (self-pay).

TOTAL TRAIL LENGTH, SURFACE & WIDTH:
1.3 miles; paved, some gravel; average 6–8' wide. Although paved, surface is uneven in places.

INCLINES & ALERTS:
There are no inclines greater than 10°. Must cross short section of road at 0.3 mile into trail and railroad tracks at 0.6 mile. Path may also be used by in-line skaters and cyclists. Dogs much be leashed. Bring your own cleanup supplies; none provided.

CONTACT:
Ashland Area Chamber of Commerce: (800) 284-9484

MILEAGE & DESCRIPTION

0.0   Trailhead begins from northeast corner of parking area to right of boat launch. Continue past beach, playground area and RV park.

Please note that you will find numerous benches throughout this entire trail. Most offer unobstructed Bay views. Of historical significance is their Timeless Timber inscription (see Foot Note, pg. 85).

0.2   Bench and accessible observation deck. The massive dock you see here is the largest structure of its kind in the world! Working operation of this dock ceased in 1965 but the informational marker gives a detailed description of it. As you continue on, there is uneven pavement and at time of writing (June 2003), a large rock blocked most of the path; however, this may have been due to construction in the area.

0.3 Continue along path and soon you will see the boathouses. Use caution as path crosses entrance road. Although these boathouses are somewhat protected, this site was hit by the very same storm that took down the Edmund Fitzgerald in 1975. Seven boathouses were destroyed at that time. The informational marker provides more detail.

0.5 Continue to follow trail to bridge (wood, double fence). This is Bay City River (Creek), which is a very old landmark of great historical significance. The informational marker is taken from the *Lake Superior County in History & Story* publication and is very intriguing. After bridge, trail surface changes to gravel and borders private property, which is marked by chainlink fence.

0.6 Cross active railroad tracks—use caution. Path changes to asphalt. There was considerable bird activity in this area and a red fox was spotted at time of writing.

0.7 This section of the Ashland Bayfront Trail ends at the Water Plant. Retrace path to trailhead.

1.3 Trailhead.

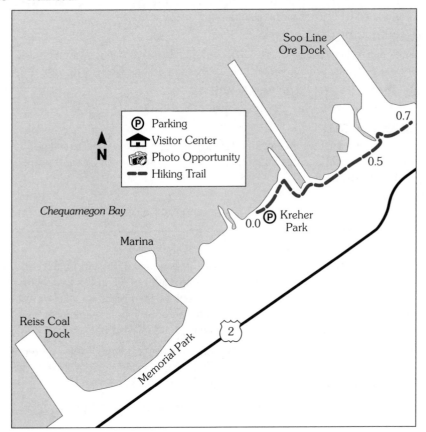

Bayview Park

On U.S. 2, 65 miles from Superior, 35 miles from Hurley

- **This entire trail is lined with well-researched interpretive signs that are worth reading. This section features an overview of an endangered species and migratory birds sightings, the Chequamegon Bay ecosystem, how Bayfield acquired its name, Ashland's railroad history and fascinating facts about Lake Superior.**

- **This trail section also has a scenic loop portion that provides picturesque views of the lovely Chequamegon Bay as well as Tern Island, which is home to an endangered tern species. A variety of birds have been sighted here, so bring the binoculars!**

TRAILHEAD DIRECTIONS & PARKING:
Located on U.S. 2, this is an easy location to find across from the shopping center. Watch for turn-in to paved parking. Ample space available in two lots. Designated wheelchair accessible parking available.

TRAILHEAD FACILITIES & FEES:
Flush toilets (wheelchair accessible), water, grills, playground, swimming beach, fishing pier, pay phone, wheelchair accessible parking. No fees for trail use.

TOTAL TRAIL LENGTH, SURFACE & WIDTH:
1.1 miles; paved, some gravel; average 6–8' wide.

INCLINES & ALERTS:
There are no inclines greater than 10°. Path may also be used by in-line skaters and cyclists. Dogs much be leashed. Bring your own cleanup supplies; none provided.

CONTACT:
Ashland Area Chamber of Commerce: (800) 284-9484

MILEAGE & DESCRIPTION

0.0 Trailhead begins from west end of west parking area. To start your journey on
  this portion of the trail, we suggest you turn left to take in the loop by the bay for very picturesque views and a closer look at Tern Island (binoculars are recommended). En route you will encounter an observation deck that is wheelchair accessible. In 300' cross abandoned railroad tracks.

Please note that you will find numerous benches throughout this entire trail. Most offer unobstructed Bay views. Of historical significance is their Timeless Timber inscription (see Foot Note, pg. 85).

0.1 At trail intersection, turn left; this begins the loop portion.

0.2 Spur to the left is an incomplete trail; stay on main trail and follow loop toward water's edge. Look for Tern Island in the distance at the end of the pilings. The Common Tern is endangered in Wisconsin. Read the interpretive marker for information about the tern's habitat as well as other birds that have been sighted here.

0.4 Upon completing this loop you will once again cross railroad tracks. Not only do birds like this area, but deer frequently graze here and may be seen on occasion. An interpretive marker contains information about the Chequamegon Bay coastal ecosystem and how this resource is managed.

0.5 Trail to right takes you to the parking area; stay on main path past picnic shelter, playground and restrooms. Just prior to picnic area is another interpretive marker that tells a fascinating story about how Bayfield acquired its name.

0.6 After passing the restrooms, use caution—the trail is interrupted by parking area. Turn left onto red brick path, which continues toward fishing pier. Take some time to read about Ashland's railroad history related in the interpretive marker here, then turn right onto gravel path. Expect this area to be lined with wildflowers during late summer.

0.8 At time of writing (June, 2003), the bench in this section was not useable due to significant overgrowth. However, the interpretive marker near the end of the trail is readable and contains some incredible facts about the greatest of the Great Lakes—Lake Superior! The fence line marks the official end of the Ashland Bayfront Trail. There are plans underway for an extension; until that time, please respect the No Trespassing sign and turn around at this point. Retrace path to trailhead.

1.1 Trailhead.

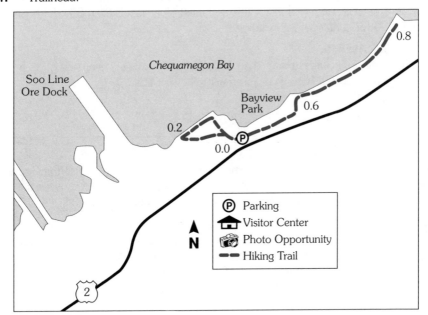

THREE BRIDGES TRAIL

Copper Falls State Park • Off U.S. 2, 64 miles from Superior, 36 miles from Hurley

- **Experience the intricate beauty of Copper Falls and rugged splendor of Brownstone Falls on this interpretive trail. These falls are wheelchair accessible and trails to them meet Universal Design Standards.**

- **See numerous scenic overlooks of the Tyler Forks Cascades and view the Bad River gorge whose walls tower 60–100'.**

- **Follow sections of the North Country National Scenic Trail as it winds through Copper Falls State Park.**

TRAILHEAD DIRECTIONS & PARKING:
From U.S. 2 in Ashland, turn south on WI 13 for 23.8 miles. Turn left (east) on County Road 169 and travel 1.7 miles to Copper Falls State Park. Turn left to park office; follow signs for Copper Falls and Brownstone Falls, which are about 1 mile beyond park office. Ample parking available in paved lot with designated wheelchair accessible parking. Separate entry routes and parking are available for those needing access to the wheelchair accessible portions of this trail (see pg. 209 for details).

TRAILHEAD FACILITIES & FEES:
Flush toilets (wheelchair accessible), water, picnic area (see Copper Falls State Park Main Picnic Area pg. 191), gift shop/concessions (seasonal). Annual or day use state park permit is required and available at park office.

TOTAL TRAIL LENGTH, SURFACE & WIDTH:
1.7 miles; cobblestone, gravel, hardpacked dirt; average 5–6' wide. Minimal rock and root. Two sections of this trail meet Universal Design Standards (see pg. 209 for additional information).

INCLINES & ALERTS:
There are no inclines greater than 10°. Steep dropoffs on river side of trail. Gorge area of Bad River is a closed area; stay on trail.

CONTACT:
Copper Falls State Park: (715) 274-5123

MILEAGE & DESCRIPTION

0.0 Trailhead begins from north corner of parking area at sign indicating Copper Falls, Brownstone Falls and Tyler Forks Cascades. Veer left around shelter following stone walkway to bridge. Descend 5 steps (stone, handrail).

0.1 Turn left to ascend 7 steps (stone, double handrail) to a very picturesque bridge (wood, double handrail). This log bridge crosses the Bad River precisely where mining activity used to take place in the park. At the end of the bridge ascend 18 steps (stone, no handrail). At trail intersection, continue straight. In this section you will encounter numerous overlooks of the Bad River.

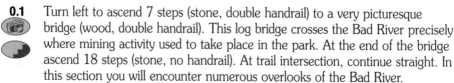

0.2 Enjoy the beautiful Copper Falls from various scenic vantage points. Shortly ascend 22 steps (stone, handrail, non-continuous). Soon you will cross a bridge (wood, double handrail).

0.3 At trail intersection turn right and enjoy the impressive stand of hemlock and glimpses into the gorge.

0.4 In this section find numerous scenic overlooks of the Bad River gorge, Tyler Forks Cascades and beautiful Brownstone Falls. At the next trail intersection, continue straight.

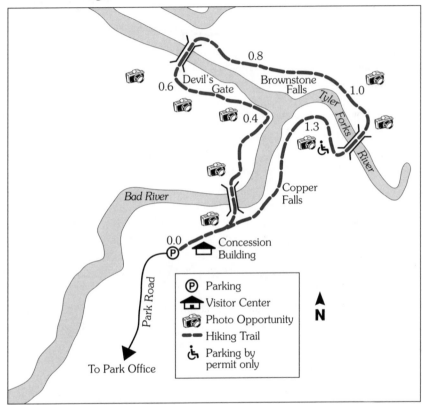

0.5 An overlook precedes a rustic sheltered bench. This is a unique place to rest. The bench bears resemblance to two pews placed back to back.

0.6 Descend 37 steps (stone, handrail); rest on the bench if you desire. Then continue down 49 steps (stone, handrail), turn the corner and continue down 36 additional steps (stone, handrail, non-continuous). In about 100' encounter a spur that leads to river's edge. The bridge ahead of you (wood, double handrail) offers views upriver of the intriguing Devil's Gate. Look for peanut brittle-like conglomerate rock here. Shortly ascend 14 steps (wood and dirt, double handrail). Turn right at sign indicating parking lot.

0.7 Ascend 87 steep steps (stone, handrail, non-continuous) to overlook.

0.8 Ascend 17 steep steps (wood and dirt, handrail). Turn right at next trail intersection. You are now on a section of the North Country National Scenic Trail (note sign), which not only runs through Copper Falls State Park but threads its way across seven states, linking over 150 parks and forests. See Foot Note below for more information.

0.9 Another covered bench in this section. Take a moment to enjoy the fresh air and beauty around you.

1.0 Take the spur trail to the right, which leads to a wooden platform offering spectacular viewing areas of the confluence of Tyler Forks and the Bad River. You will need to ascend and descend 34 steps (wood, double handrail, non-continuous) to access these overlooks. Alert: Steep dropoffs on river side; no guardrails. Tyler Forks River is named after the Great Lakes ship captain John Tyler. For other interesting info about the park, pick up the free Visitor newspaper from park office.

1.1 At intersection, turn right and cross bridge (wood, double handrail). This is a great place for viewing the Bad River.

1.2 Turn right at end of bridge and follow sign indicating parking lot. This section affords lovely glimpses of the Bad River. Alert: Steep dropoffs on river side; no guardrails. At next intersection, continue straight. Trail to left takes you to vault toilets and wheelchair accessible parking; however, you must have a valid handicapped parking permit to use this parking area (see pg. 209 for additional information). Beyond this point, the trail splits and rejoins in 100'; trail to right hugs the river.

1.3 Ascend 6 steps (stone, handrail) and continue to overlook with spectacular view of Brownstone Falls and Bad River gorge. Trail splits; path to the left is the park's wheelchair designated trail. Stay right.

1.4 Wheelchair accessible trail rejoins from the left; go straight.

1.5 Bridge affords another viewing opportunity of Copper Falls. This bridge is noteworthy because for the first time persons using wheelchairs can view Copper Falls. Soon you will descend 27 steps (stone, handrail).

1.6 Ascend 14 steps (stone, no handrail, non-continuous). Nice view of the river is available here. As you approach the shelter, notice a bench to the left. You might want to go the concession stand and purchase a refreshing scoop of your favorite ice cream. Clearly some of the best ice cream we've tasted. Rumor has it the authors may have driven all the way from Duluth for a cone!

1.7 Trailhead.

The North Country National Scenic Trail runs through Copper Falls State Park and links outstanding scenic, natural, recreational, historic and cultural areas spanning a seven state region: North Dakota, Minnesota, Wisconsin, Michigan, Ohio, Pennsylvania and New York and is primarily maintained by volunteers. For more information visit www.northcountrytrail.org.

Brownstone Falls. Photo by Ladona Tornabene

OBSERVATION TOWER

Copper Falls State Park • Off U.S. 2, 64 miles from Superior, 36 miles from Hurley

- **Originally built in 1937, this tower provides incredible panoramic views of Chequamegon-Nicolet National Forest to the south and west. On a clear day, the Apostle Islands and Lake Superior's Chequamegon Bay may be visible to the north.**

TRAILHEAD DIRECTIONS & PARKING:

From U.S. 2 in Ashland, turn south on WI 13 for 23.8 miles. Turn left (east) on County Road 169 and travel 1.7 miles to Copper Falls State Park. Turn left and follow signs for Copper Falls and Brownstone Falls, which are about 1 mile beyond park office. Ample parking available in paved lot with designated wheelchair accessible parking.

TRAILHEAD FACILITIES & FEES:

Flush toilets (wheelchair accessible), water, picnic area (see Copper Falls State Park Main Picnic Area pg. 191), gift shop/concessions (seasonal). Annual or day use state park permit is required and available at park office.

TOTAL TRAIL LENGTH, SURFACE & WIDTH:

0.7 mile; cobblestone, gravel, hardpacked dirt; average 4–6' wide. Minimal rock and root.

INCLINES & ALERTS:

There are three inclines ranging from 12–16°. Steepest is 16° for 10' at 0.2 mile. Unsecured logs laid to facilitate crossing some wet areas. Steep cliffs, erosion in places; no guardrail.

CONTACT:

Copper Falls State Park: (715) 274-5123

MILEAGE & DESCRIPTION

0.0 Trailhead begins from north corner of parking area at sign indicating Copper Falls, Brownstone Falls and Tyler Forks Cascades. Veer left around shelter following stone walkway to bridge. Descend 5 steps (stone, handrail).

0.1 Turn left to ascend 7 steps (stone, double handrail) to a very picturesque bridge (wood, double handrail). This log bridge crosses the Bad River precisely where mining activity used to take place in the park. At the end of the bridge ascend 18 steps (stone, no handrail). At trail intersection, turn left and continue up hill following sign indicating Observation Tower. Begin ascent of 142 steps (wood, double handrail, non-continuous)

0.2 This section contains a short laid log path—use caution. It also contains the area of steepest incline (16° for 10').

0.3 At trail intersection, turn right and continue to tower base.

0.4 Ascend 75 steps (wood, double handrail) to top of tower for an incredible panoramic view of woodlands and, on a clear day, the Apostle Islands and Lake Superior's Chequamegon Bay. This tower, which was originally built in 1937, has been rebuilt within the last 12 years. When ready, retrace path to trailhead.

0.7 Trailhead.

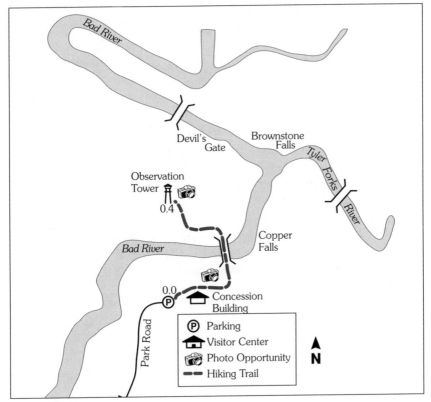

 SAYS WHO?

Have trouble drinking enough? (Water, that is!)

Studies show that some people have an easier time drinking sports drinks than water during physical activity because sports drinks taste good.

Appetite [50]

RED GRANITE FALLS TRAIL

Copper Falls State Park • Off U.S. 2, 64 miles from Superior, 36 miles from Hurley

- **This is a gorgeous wooded hike that parallels a portion of the Bad River.**
- **Look for impressive stand of hemlock along river bank.**

TRAILHEAD DIRECTIONS & PARKING:
From U.S. 2 in Ashland, turn south on WI 13 for 23.8 miles. Turn left (east) on County Road 169 and travel 1.7 miles to Copper Falls State Park. Turn left and follow signs for Red Granite Falls Trail, which is located just a short distance beyond park office. Ample parking available with designated wheelchair accessible parking.

TRAILHEAD FACILITIES & FEES:
Flush toilets (wheelchair accessible), water, small picnic area and beach house. Annual or day use state park permit is required and available at park office.

TOTAL TRAIL LENGTH, SURFACE & WIDTH:
2.4 miles; gravel, hardpacked dirt, grass; average 3–4' wide (contingent on mowing). Minimal rock and root.

INCLINES & ALERTS:
There is one incline of 14° for 35' at 0.9 mile. Even though there is only one incline over 10°, this is not a flat trail but is gently rolling. No trash containers; pack in & pack out. Must cross access road 135' into trail.

CONTACT:
Copper Falls State Park: (715) 274-5123

MILEAGE & DESCRIPTION

0.0 Trailhead begins from southeast corner of parking area off asphalt path near sign indicating Red Granite Falls Trail. Proceed through small picnic area, then cross access road.

0.3 At trail intersection turn right and follow sign indicating Red Granite Falls. At next intersection, continue straight. Throughout this trail you will observe many hemlock. This tree is dominant in and typical of this area but not so in other areas of Northern Wisconsin.

0.5 At trail intersection, turn right.

0.8 Here you will enter open field and cross under power line right-of-way.

0.9 At intersection, continue straight following marker. Shortly, the Bad River rushes into view. This bank is lined by a beautiful stand of hemlock. This river originates in Caroline Lake, which is located in east central Ashland County, and runs a meandering course northward until its point of dispersion—Lake Superior. For more interesting facts pick up the Copper Falls State Park Visitor newspaper, free at park office.

In 600' you will encounter the area of steepest incline (14° for 35').

1.1 At next intersection, turn right. Soon you will again cross power line right-of-way.

1.5 Grassy area; trail width is contingent on mowing.

1.8 At trail intersection continue straight. At next intersection turn right and follow sign for parking lot.

2.1 Turn right at next trail intersection and follow parking lot sign. Retrace path to trailhead.

2.4 Trailhead.

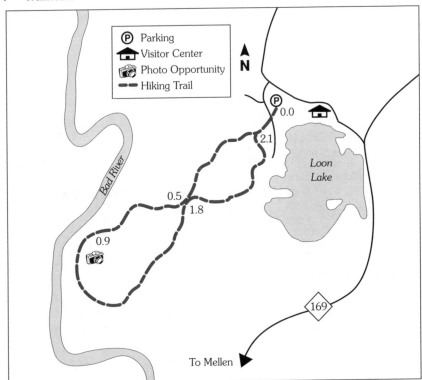

 Foot Note:

"Just a few thousand years ago, Lake Superior held so much water that it was high enough to leave old beach lines in Copper Falls State Park!"

Source: Copper Falls State Park Visitor

MORGAN FALLS

Chequamegon-Nicolet National Forest • Off U.S. 2, 64 miles from Superior, 36 miles from Hurley

- **Picturesque Morgan Falls tumbles 70' over jagged granite face.**
- **Late spring hiking may afford spectacular views of large trillium.**

TRAILHEAD DIRECTIONS & PARKING:

From U.S. 2 in Ashland, turn south on WI 13 for 14.4 miles. Turn right (west) on County Road C and travel 4.7 miles to stop sign. Continue straight for another 1.2 miles until you come to County Line Road (Ashland/Bayfield). Turn left (south) on this gravel road for 3.9 miles. You will find a gravel parking lot on the left side.

TRAILHEAD FACILITIES, & FEES:

Vault toilet (wheelchair accessible; however, at time of writing (June 2003) there was a 5–6" step outside the toilet). U.S. Forest vehicle stickers are required to park in this lot or day use fee of $3 (self-pay). Maps are available.

TOTAL TRAIL LENGTH, SURFACE & WIDTH:

1.1 miles; gravel, hardpacked dirt; average 4–6' wide. Minimal rock and root.

INCLINES & ALERTS:

There are no inclines greater than 10°. Please do not leave the trail or climb the cliffs in the Morgan Creek area. Muddy areas possible.

CONTACT:

Chequamegon-Nicolet National Forest: (715) 264-2511

MILEAGE & DESCRIPTION

0.0 Trailhead begins from SE corner of parking lot nearest toilet. Cross bridge (wood, no handrails) over picturesque creek as you enter a lovely fern glade. You will cross two more bridges in this section (wood, no handrail). Before crossing third bridge, turn left at trail intersection.

0.1 At next trail intersection turn left. In about 700' cross fourth bridge (wood, no handrail).

0.3 When you arrive at next intersection turn left. Soon you will cross a fifth bridge (wood, no handrail), this one over a small creek. At following intersection turn right.

0.4 Look left and you will see the remnants of an old brick fireplace. This was from the CCC campground in the 1930s. At intersection, turn right. Listen closely. Can you hear the sound of the falls? Cross sixth bridge (wood, no handrail) over Morgan Creek. Trail follows along creek.

0.5 Cross seventh bridge (wood, no handrail).

0.6 Path to picturesque Morgan Falls. Morgan Falls is located on the western end of the Penokee Range. The Falls are nice and lend themselves to some creative photo ops from the base. Spend a little time here and when ready, retrace path to trailhead.

1.1 Trailhead.

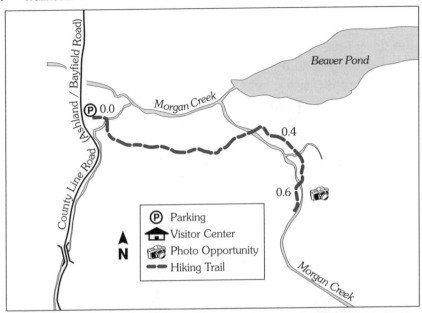

Morgan Falls. Photo by Melanie Morgan

POTATO RIVER—UPPER FALLS

Off U.S. 2, 85 miles from Superior, 15 miles from Hurley

- **See Upper Falls—a series of 3 gorgeous cascades framed beautifully by rock face. Remember your camera!**
- **See Lower Falls, which is larger and framed by the forest.**
- **Spectacular drive en route to these falls.**

TRAILHEAD DIRECTIONS & PARKING:
From U.S. 2, turn south on WI 169. Drive 2.7 miles to sign for Potato River Falls Road (0.5 mile past narrow underpass). Turn right and travel on gravel road 1.3 miles to picnic area. Park in gravel loop.

TRAILHEAD FACILITIES & FEES:
Vault toilets (wheelchair accessible), grills, open-sided shelter, picnic area. No fees for trail use.

TOTAL TRAIL LENGTH, SURFACE & WIDTH:
0.3 mile; hardpacked dirt, gravel; average 3–4' wide. Minimal rock and root.

INCLINES & ALERTS:
There are no inclines greater than 10°. Spur trails are very steep and eroded; stay on the main path. Stair treads vary.

CONTACT:
Iron County Development Zone Council: (715) 561-2922

MILEAGE & DESCRIPTION

0.0   View of Upper Falls begins at south end of picnic area at sign indicating same. Stay on the main trail as spurs are steep and eroded.

0.1   You can hear the falls in the distance as you begin to descend the 131 steps (wood, double handrail, non-continuous) and continue to viewing area. The observation deck offers an excellent view of the cascades and the Potato River Upper Falls. The falls are extremely scenic and can yield some fabulous photos. Spend some time here. When ready, retrace path to trailhead.

0.2   For an easy view of Lower Falls begin at west side of picnic area at sign indicating Observation Deck. Descend a 4–6'-wide hardpacked dirt and gravel path to the viewing area. This path is not level due to erosion. Here you will find a partial view of Lower Falls, depending upon foliage. Although this is the larger of the falls, you may want a telephoto lens to capture it. Definitely worth seeing and hearing. When ready, retrace path to trailhead.

0.3   Trailhead.

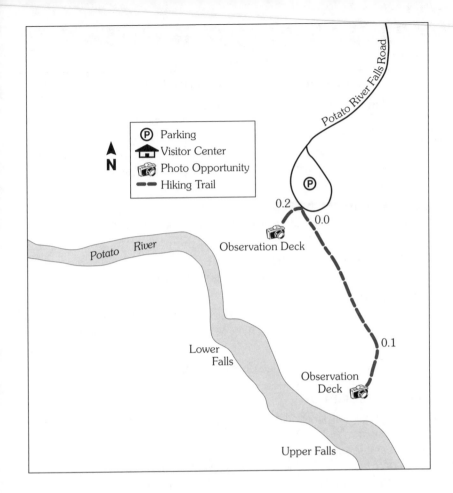

Map legend:
- ⓟ Parking
- 🏠 Visitor Center
- 📷 Photo Opportunity
- ▬ ▬ Hiking Trail

N

Potato River Falls Road

ⓟ

0.2

0.0

Observation Deck

Potato River

0.1

Lower Falls

Observation Deck

Upper Falls

 Foot Note:

For more information about the many waterfalls of Wisconsin, we strongly recommend the book *Wisconsin Waterfalls* (see Appendix A).

POTATO RIVER—LOWER FALLS

Off U.S. 2, 85 miles from Superior, 15 miles from Hurley

- **A closer and more magnificent view of Lower Falls.**
- **Spectacular drive en route to these falls.**

TRAILHEAD DIRECTIONS & PARKING:
From U.S. 2, turn south on WI 169. Drive 2.7 miles to sign for Potato River Falls Road (0.5 mile past narrow underpass). Turn right and travel on gravel road 1.3 miles to picnic area. Park in gravel loop.

TRAILHEAD FACILITIES & FEES:
Vault toilets (wheelchair accessible), grills, open-sided shelter, picnic area. No fees for trail use.

TOTAL TRAIL LENGTH, SURFACE & WIDTH:
0.4 mile; hardpacked dirt, gravel; average 3–4' wide. Minimal rock and root.

INCLINES & ALERTS:
There are no inclines greater than 10°. Some overgrowth possible. Stair treads vary. Water level at river bottom may be high due to heavy rainfall.

CONTACT:
Iron County Development Zone Council: (715) 561-2922

MILEAGE & DESCRIPTION

0.0 At beginning of parking loop find sign indicating Trail to River, Lower Falls. If you have trouble locating it, look way to the right of sign for Observation Deck and toward beginning of park loop. Enter on hardpacked dirt path. You will descend the following series of steps (74, 16, 34; wood, single handrail, non-continuous) before arriving at the viewing platform.

0.1 This deck gives a somewhat different perspective of the lower falls. Enjoy the view from the bench. If you decide to hike to the river bottom, continue to follow the path around the viewing deck. You will descend another series of steps (68, 13, 6; wood, single or double handrail, non-continuous). When you arrive at a bend in the trail just above the river, do not scramble down here but turn right and go a short distance; descend another 12 steps (wood, handrail).

0.2 Continue to the river bottom or continue approximately 300' to the bend in the river. This is quite picturesque, but water level may be high due to spring runoff or heavy rains. Use caution. Retrace path to trailhead.

0.4 Trailhead.

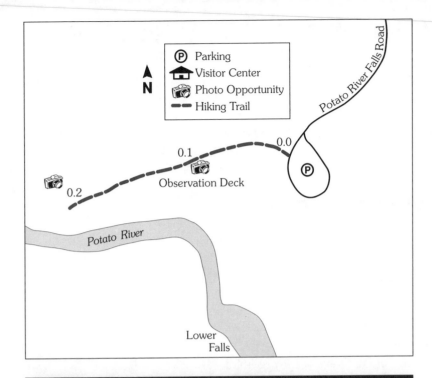

Parking
Visitor Center
Photo Opportunity
Hiking Trail

N

Potato River Falls Road

0.0

0.1

0.2

Observation Deck

Potato River

Lower
Falls

Upper Falls of Potato River. Photo by Ladona Tornabene

Twin Falls Park, Port Wing • On WI 13, 42 miles from Superior, 56 miles from Ashland

- **You won't want to miss the beauty to be found in this small, local park.**
- **Striking view into a small gorge and lovely hidden falls.**

TRAILHEAD DIRECTIONS & PARKING:

From WI 13 on west side of Port Wing, south side of road, turn at sign indicating Twin Falls Park (Fire #8605). Follow in-drive around circle. Park near small white building or in cut-through area.

TRAILHEAD FACILITIES & FEES:

Picnic table and grill nearby. No fees for trail use.

TOTAL TRAIL LENGTH, SURFACE & WIDTH:

0.4 mile; grass, hardpacked dirt; average 4–6' wide. Minimal rock and root.

INCLINES & ALERTS:

There are no inclines greater than 10°. Steep cliffs in places; stay on trail. Part of the trail follows in-drive. Trail borders private property—stay on designated path.

CONTACT:

Town of Port Wing: (715) 774-3695

MILEAGE & DESCRIPTION

0.0   Trailhead begins at sign indicating Winter Green Trail, which can be accessed from circle in-drive not far from the small white building. You will walk along a fence line as you continue on trail before reaching the observation deck.

0.1   Two steps up take you to an observation deck with a striking view of a small gorge. Look to left; tucked under a cedar find Upper Falls. Lower Falls is located directly under the observation deck. The steps you see on the other side are on private property. To see Lower Falls, you would need to hike in the creek over many large boulders; that access route fell outside the parameters of this book.

As you leave the observation deck you will see a sign indicating Ravine Bottom Trail. You may take this if you desire as this trail intersects Top Ridge Trail in 400'; however, we recommend the more scenic route. To access this route, continue uphill past sign indicating Ravine Bottom. At Y turn left on grassy path as trail turns away from the gorge. At top of rise you will find a sign indicating Top Ridge Trail; take that to the left. Path to the right was extremely overgrown at time of writing.

0.2   Enter dramatic stand of fir and watch for orange ties on trees to mark path. At time of writing, someone had laid tree branches to mark the trail. Continue to follow trail until it ends at park road near parking area.

0.4   Trailhead.

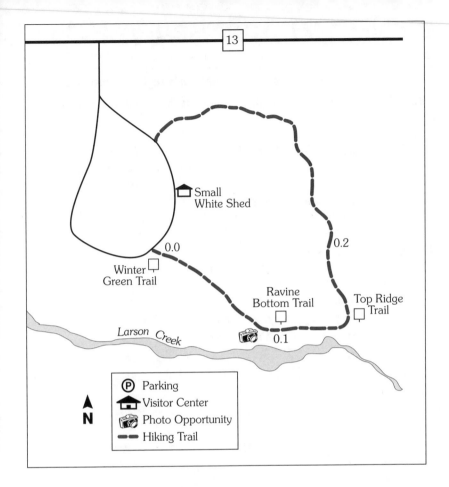

Small
White Shed

0.0

0.2

Winter
Green Trail

Ravine
Bottom Trail

Top Ridge
Trail

Larson Creek

0.1

▲
N

(P) Parking
🏠 Visitor Center
📷 Photo Opportunity
▬▬ Hiking Trail

 SAYS WHO?

In a bad mood? Stride toward a better attitude!

Walking 30 minutes 4-6 days per week at a moderate pace can improve attitude, mood, self esteem and feelings of well-being.

Exercising Your Way to Better Mental Health [44,42,43,27,25,26]

POINT TRAIL/LOOP (SOUTH)

Big Bay State Park, Madeline Island • Off WI 13, 78 miles from Superior, 20 miles from Ashland

- **Incredibly scenic overlooks of Lake Superior's rugged shoreline.**
- **Beautiful wooded hike through the heart of the forest offers tranquility for the soul.**

TRAILHEAD DIRECTIONS & PARKING:

From Ferry Dock on Main Street turn right. Drive two blocks to Middle Road (note brown sign for Big Bay State Park); turn left. Travel 4 miles to stop sign (road name then changes to Hagen Road). Continue straight for 2 miles and turn left to park office. Head east toward Outdoor Group Camp. Parking is available at Overlook Area. Designated wheelchair accessible parking available.

TRAILHEAD FACILITIES & FEES:

Picnic tables and bicycle rack. Flush toilets (wheelchair accessible) and water available at park office nearby. Annual or day use state park permit is required and is available at the park office.

TOTAL TRAIL LENGTH, SURFACE & WIDTH:

1.9 miles; hardpacked dirt and gravel; average 2–4' wide.

INCLINES & ALERTS:

There are no inclines greater than 10°. Steep cliffs—stay on trail. All overlooks are officially marked by wooden fences.

CONTACT:

Big Bay State Park: (715) 747-6425

MILEAGE & DESCRIPTION

0.0 Trailhead begins at east end of parking near bike rack at sign indicating "Point Trail." Immediately experience the breathtaking beauty of Lake Superior and her rugged cliff face! At 100' you will find a spur to the right along the fence line. We recommend taking it as it rejoins the main trail. The views of Lake Superior are exceptional.

In approximately 100', a spur to the left leads to an outdoor group camp. Please respect privacy and continue straight ahead on trail.

0.1 Another beautiful overlook of the lake. Directly opposite overlook is a new trail. At time of writing (August 2003) this trail was not yet complete. Please consult park office for current information.

0.2 This overlook of Lake Superior's shoreline is simply magnificent. A visual feast anytime but auditory as well if waves are crashing on the rocky face.

0.3 This overlook features another rocky shoreline view—incredible!

0.4 This is where the loop portion of the trail rejoins the main trail. You will return on this path, but for now stay on main trail close to the lake and along fence line. Shortly you will find a trail map and sign indicating "Point Trail 1 mile" and in another 200', a great stand of hemlock.

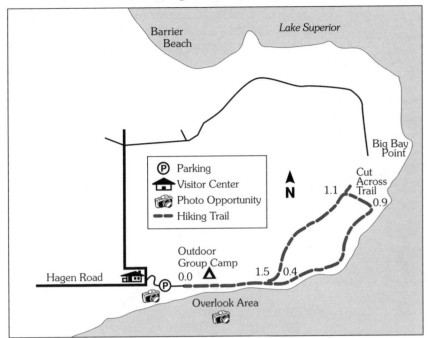

0.9 Find sign to the left indicating "Cut Across Trail", which signals the beginning of the interpretive section of this trail. We strongly recommend turning left and taking the loop through this incredibly peaceful wooded area. Trail does continue straight for another 0.2 mile to Big Bay Point overlook (see Point Trail/Loop (North) pg. 114), but for now take the interpretive loop.

Marker #1 "Yellow Birch." The yellow birch often grows with hemlock. They are very prominent members of Wisconsin's hardwood forests.

Marker #2 "White Birch." The white birch often grows in clumps. Read about the many uses of its bark.

Marker #3 "Northern White Cedar." Discover why it is called the Tree of Life.

1.0 Marker # 4 "Red Oak." Red oak is the most common oak in northern Wisconsin and the fastest growing. Wisconsin has 7 oak species.

Marker #5 "Sugar Maple." Famous for its maple syrup, this tree has three qualities that give it great importance in a forest: High reproduction rate, shade tolerance and long life. Think about this next time you top your pancakes with the sweet syrup!

Marker #6 "Red Maple." Not famous for maple syrup, but still tops the forest with its crimson red color in the fall.

Marker #7 "Eastern Hemlock." The hemlocks are slow growers. Animals of the forest enjoy fine dining at this tree and this marker reveals some of their menu choices.

1.1 At trail intersection, turn left (trail to the right is part of Point Trail/Loop (North) pg. 114). Although the interpretive portion ends, the beauty doesn't as this section takes you through the heart of the forest. While walking this part of the trail, see how many trees you can now identify after reading the interpretive section.

1.5 Trail intersection at fence line concludes the loop portion of this hike. Veer right and retrace path to trailhead. Be sure to stop at the overlooks again for a different view!

1.9 Trailhead

 SAYS WHO?

Want to get smart? Work out the heart!

Walking improves the functioning of the brain.

American Fitness [45]

Point Trail/Loop (South). Photo by Lisa Vogelsang

POINT TRAIL/LOOP (NORTH)

Big Bay State Park, Madeline Island • Off WI 13, 78 miles from Superior, 20 miles from Ashland

- **Wonderful views of Lake Superior's rugged shoreline.**

- **Beautiful wooded hike through an old growth forest featuring hemlocks that are 200–300 years old!**

TRAILHEAD DIRECTIONS & PARKING:

From Ferry Dock on Main Street turn right. Drive two blocks to Middle Road (note brown sign for Big Bay State Park); turn left. Travel 4 miles to stop sign (road name then changes to Hagen Road). Continue straight for 2 miles and turn left to park office. At first park stop sign turn right toward Campground, Picnic Area and Beach. At next stop sign turn right toward Big Bay Point. Continue on road past Picnic Area and Beach to paved parking loop. Wheelchair accessible parking, moped parking and bike racks available.

TRAILHEAD FACILITIES & FEES:

Vault toilets (wheelchair accessible), water, Big Bay Point Picnic Area (pg. 194). Annual or day use state park permit is required and is available at the park office.

TOTAL TRAIL LENGTH, SURFACE & WIDTH:

0.5 mile; hardpacked dirt and gravel; average 2–5' wide.

INCLINES & ALERTS:

There are no inclines greater than 10°. Steep cliffs—stay on trail. All overlooks are officially marked by wooden fences.

CONTACT:

Big Bay State Park: (715) 747-6425

MILEAGE & DESCRIPTION

0.0 Trailhead begins at east end of parking area near self pay box. Enter through an old growth forest and into a gorgeous stand of hemlock (some are 200–300 years old!). You will find several picnic tables scattered about. In 150' restrooms will be to the left. At time of writing there was a very intriguing sight just prior to trail intersection near a picnic table toward the right. Branches had been woven together to form a hut-like structure under a tree. If still there, it's worth a look

0.1 Trail intersection to the left is Bay View Trail (pg. 118). Continue straight and find sign indicating "Point Trail 1.5 mile" on the right. However, before taking that trail, continue straight 100' to the overlook marked by a wooden fence. This is Big Bay Point and offers a grand view of Lake Superior's rugged shoreline and cliffs. There is also a unique stone bench on the point that is very picturesque. After spending some time at the Point, proceed to the Point Trail.

0.3 Find overlook of stone ledge undercut by Lake Superior's wave action. Very nice scenery. In approximately 200', note sign on left indicating "Cut Across Trail" and map. Turn right (trail does continue straight for another 0.9 mile; see Point Trail/Loop (South) pg. 110), but for now take the loop as this is the interpretive section of the trail and leads to an incredibly peaceful wooded area.

Marker #1 "Yellow Birch." The yellow birch often grows with hemlock. They are very prominent members of Wisconsin's hardwood forests.

Marker #2 "White Birch." The white birch often grows in clumps. Read about the many uses of its bark.

Marker #3 "Northern White Cedar." Discover why it is called the Tree of Life.

Marker # 4 "Red Oak." Red oak is the most common oak in northern Wisconsin and the fastest growing. Wisconsin has 7 oak species.

Marker #5 "Sugar Maple." Famous for its maple syrup, this tree has three qualities that give it great importance in a forest: High reproduction rate, shade tolerance and long life. Think about this next time you top your pancakes with the sweet syrup!

Marker #6 "Red Maple." Not famous for maple syrup, but still tops the forest with its crimson red color in the fall.

Marker #7 "Eastern Hemlock." The hemlocks are slow growers. Animals of the forest enjoy fine dining at this tree and this marker reveals some of their menu choices.

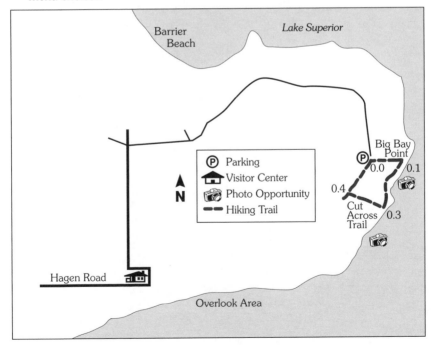

0.4 This ends the interpretive section of the trail. Find sign indicating "Cut Across Trail" and turn right (trail to the left is part of Point Trail/Loop (South), pg. 110). Pause here and let the stillness refresh you.

0.5 Parking area and trailhead.

 SAYS WHO?

Still trying to kick the habit? Take a walk.

Exercise has been shown to aid people who are trying to quit smoking. They report fewer cravings as well as a reduction in the amount of smoking they do.

Archives of Internal Medicine [34,18]

Point Trail/Loop (North). Photo by Lisa Vogelsang

BAY VIEW TRAIL

Big Bay State Park, Madeline Island • Off WI 13, 78 miles from Superior, 20 miles from Ashland

- **Beautiful vista of the Big Bay of Lake Superior and east side of Madeline Island.**
- **Nice views of Lake Superior throughout.**
- **Opportunity to see an abandoned eagle's nest.**

TRAILHEAD DIRECTIONS & PARKING:

From Ferry Dock on Main Street turn right. Drive two blocks to Middle Road (note brown sign indicating Big Bay State Park); turn left. Travel 4 miles to stop sign (road name then changes to Hagen Road). Continue straight for 2 miles and turn left to park office. At first park stop sign turn right toward Campground, Picnic Area and Beach. At next stop sign turn right toward Big Bay Point. Continue on road past Picnic Area and Beach to paved parking loop. Wheelchair accessible parking, moped parking and bike racks available.

TRAILHEAD FACILITIES & FEES:

Vault toilets (wheelchair accessible) 150' into trail, water, Big Bay Point Picnic Area (see pg. 194). Annual or day use state park permit is required and is available at the park office.

TOTAL TRAIL LENGTH, SURFACE & WIDTH:

2.3 miles; hardpacked dirt and gravel; average 2–5' wide.

INCLINES & ALERTS:

There are no inclines greater than 10°. Steep cliffs—stay on trail. All overlooks are officially marked by wooden fences. At time of writing (August 2003), trail was hikeable but being rerouted due to erosion problems. Contact park office for current information.

CONTACT:

Big Bay State Park: (715) 747-6425

MILEAGE & DESCRIPTION

0.0 Trailhead begins at east end of parking area near self pay box. Enter through an old growth forest and into a gorgeous stand of hemlock (some are 200–300 years old!). You will find several picnic tables scattered about. In 150' restrooms will be to the left. At time of writing there was a very intriguing sight just prior to trail intersection near a picnic table toward the right. Branches had been woven together to form a hut-like structure under a tree. If still there, it's worth a look.

0.1 At trail intersection to the left find sign indicating "Bay View Trail 1.3 miles." However, before taking that trail, continue straight to the overlook marked by a wooden fence. This is Big Bay Point and offers a grand view of Lake Superior's rugged shoreline and cliffs. There is also a unique stone bench on the point that is very picturesque. After spending some time at the Point, proceed to the Bay View Trail.

0.4 You'll cross two bridges (wood, double handrail) in this section, approximately 200' apart. After the second bridge, the abandoned eagle's nest is about 300' to the right and perched high in a large aspen tree. The park closed this trail while the eagles were there. Continue along trail and cross two additional bridges (wood, double handrail).

1.0 By now you may have noticed numerous trees down along this trail. A marker to the left gives information about the blowdown that hit this area hard on June 27, 1991. Winds exceeding 100 mph swept through here. Just opposite this site is a striking vista of Big Bay and the east side of Madeline Island, as well as the park's 1.5 miles of beach area. Find a log that has been strategically placed here to serve as the only bench on this trail.

1.2 Another bridge (wood, double handrail) brings you to the end of this trail and into the open field of Barrier Beach Picnic Area (pg. 193). Beach access is nearby (see Barrier Beach Almost Hike pg. 168). Retrace path to trailhead.

2.3 Trailhead.

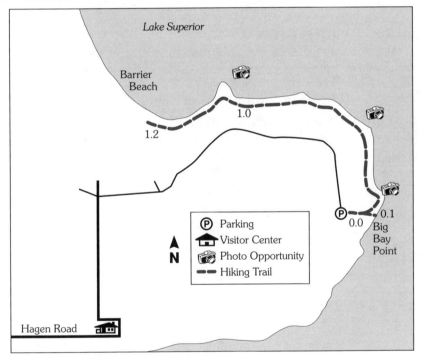

Lake Superior

Barrier Beach

1.0

1.2

P) Parking
Visitor Center
Photo Opportunity
Hiking Trail

N

0.0 0.1
Big Bay Point

Hagen Road

Foot Note:

This is a popular trail that the Bus Tour offers as its hike at Big Bay State Park. For more information about this tour see Foot Note for Barrier Beach Almost Hike (pg. 168).

Big Bay State Park, Madeline Island • Off WI 13, 78 miles from Superior, 20 miles from Ashland

- **Spectacular views of Lake Superior and Barrier Beach area!**
- **A beautiful stroll along boardwalk offers access to a portion of the 1.5 miles of beach within Big Bay State Park.**
- **First 0.5 mile of boardwalk is interpretive.**

TRAILHEAD DIRECTIONS & PARKING:

From Ferry Dock on Main Street turn right. Drive two blocks to Middle Road (note brown sign for Big Bay State Park); turn left. Travel 4 miles to stop sign (road name then changes to Hagen Road). Continue straight for 2 miles and turn left to park office. At first park stop sign turn right toward Campground, Picnic Area and Beach. At next stop sign turn right toward Picnic Area and Beach, then left to Barrier Beach and paved parking lot. Wheelchair accessible parking, moped parking and bike racks available.

TRAILHEAD FACILITIES & FEES:

Vault toilets (wheelchair accessible), water, changing stalls, fire ring, benches, naturalist/environmental programs (see kiosk near blue shed for schedules), picnic area (see Barrier Beach Picnic Area pg. 193). Annual or day use state park permit is required and is available at the park office.

TOTAL TRAIL LENGTH, SURFACE & WIDTH:

2.9 miles; boardwalk, hardpacked dirt and gravel, paved; average 5' wide.

INCLINES & ALERTS:

There are no inclines greater than 10°. No bicycles allowed on boardwalk (a rack is provided near trailhead for your convenience). Pets are not permitted as this trail is near the beach area. No lifeguard on duty. Occasional overgrowth on boardwalk may be problematic in summer. Due to very fragile vegetation, please stay on boardwalk sections at all times.

CONTACT:

Big Bay State Park: (715) 747-6425

MILEAGE & DESCRIPTION

0.0   Trailhead begins on paved path at north end of parking area toward restrooms. Behind restrooms, walk left through open field toward the blue naturalist shed and fire ring to find sign indicating "Boardwalk to Barrier Beach." Near the informational kiosk will be a small box containing free brochures regarding bird, wildflower and fern identification in addition to park maps. The informational kiosk also posts schedules of naturalist/environmental programs. Path turns to gravel and hardpacked dirt.

0.1   At trail intersection, turn right and head toward beach area on 5'-wide paved path.

0.2 Here you will find a bench and Marker #1 "Map." This is the first of 12 interpretive markers on this trail. Straight ahead lies a spectacular view of Lake Superior and Barrier Beach! This area offers beach access and is a popular swimming spot in summer. The sandy beach also hosts many weathered logs that have been naturally sculpted by water and sand yielding some creative photo ops. These logs also provide makeshift benches for enjoying the beauty of this spot.

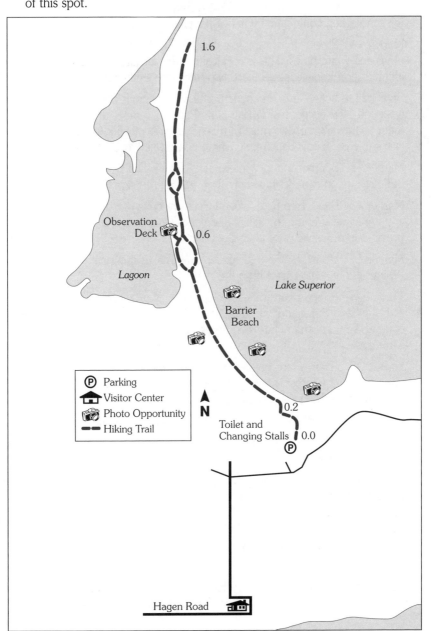

Turn left onto boardwalk to access the remainder of this trail. Shortly you will find Marker #2 "Tree and Plant Survivors." The trees and plants throughout this trail have adapted to survive under severe conditions such as shifting sands, nutrient-poor soil, strong winds and deep snow, yet remain very sensitive to one environmental factor—us. Please stay on boardwalk at all times.

Marker #3 "White Birch." White birch are the first trees to grow after a forest fire. Their bark is waterproof and rot resistant, hence the reason it was used for canoes and containers by native peoples.

Marker #4 "Pines." Information is given to help you distinguish between red pines and white pines. This is an ideal trail for locating both and testing your identification knowledge as these two trees frequently appear side by side.

0.3 Spur trail to beach area and bench. Official spur trails are composed of boardwalk and offer access to Big Bay State Park's 1.5 miles of sandy beach. The main boardwalk parallels most of this beach area yielding gorgeous lake views. Please access beach only where boardwalk has been laid.

Marker #5 "Bearberry and Wintergreen." These two plants flourish along this trail. See if you can identify each after reading this sign.

Marker #6 "Dead Tree Role." Dead trees are quite essential to the ecosystem and are actually home to wildlife and various plant species. Another bench provides glorious views of Lake Superior.

Marker #7 "Dwarf Juniper." Discover what makes this such a hearty plant. Where else have you seen it on the trail?

0.4 Three benches and boardwalk spur to beach. Shortly you will enter the Big Bay Sand Spit and Bog State Natural Area. This boreal forest lowland contains some of the richest bog floras in the Lake Superior region. Use with care.

Marker #8 "Forest Floor Layer." Read about the ingredients that make up the forest floor. The forest is especially efficient as every particle plays a role in the survival of the dune complex.

0.5 Bench with view of forest as the trail turns away from Lake Superior.

Marker #9 "Huckleberry and Blueberry." Learn to distinguish between these two sweet berries.

Marker #10 "Reindeer Moss." OK, you won't see any reindeer or a sleigh but white-tailed deer sightings are a real possibility! Actually, this plant is really a lichen. Lichens are the first plants to grow on a surface and the area you see here sports an abundance of reindeer lichen.

Soon the boardwalk creates a loop marked by a bench. Veer left and head toward lagoon.

Marker #11 "Speckled Alder." Alders make life easier for other plants and play an important role in the forest. See marker for more information.

0.6 Bench provides a lovely view of Big Bay Lagoon. Another bench marks the spur to the lagoon. Turn left and in 100' find an observation deck where yet another bench provides a perfect spot for capturing the serenity of this place. While picturesque at any time, this would be a marvelous place to catch a sunset. Contrast the calmness of the lagoon with Lake Superior on a windy day.

Marker #12 "Map of trail" and summary of how plants thrive under harsh conditions yet remain sensitive to people (a gentle reminder to stay on the boardwalk). This officially ends the interpretive section of the trail. At this intersection, you have three options. Straight ahead is a boardwalk spur with bench that provides a great view of the lake and Big Bay. Path to the right leads back to trailhead; path to the left takes you on another 0.9 mile extension of boardwalk through the forest with spurs leading to magnificent Lake Superior views and beach access. The boardwalk will eventually end and trail becomes hardpacked dirt, then turns to soft sand culminating at Big Bay Town Park and mouth of lagoon.

Note: To honor our book criteria for trail length, we end our description of this trail where the boardwalk ends; however, we do approach the nonboardwalk portion of the trail from Big Bay Town Park Trail (see pg. 128).

If you choose to continue on the remaining 0.9 mile of boardwalk expect to find another loop area, seven more benches (some with spectacular Superior views, others with wooded views) as well as boardwalk spurs leading to beach access. We found the beach area less crowded in this section.

1.6 End of boardwalk. The trail continues for another 0.4 mile (see Big Bay Town Park Trail pg. 128). However, to complete this section of the hike while staying under 3 miles, turn around and follow boardwalk (omitting spur trails and loops) to trailhead.

2.9 Trailhead.

Boardwalk Interpretive Trail. Photo by Melanie Morgan

LAGOON RIDGE TRAIL

Big Bay State Park, Madeline Island • Off WI 13, 78 miles from Superior, 20 miles from Ashland

- **A solitary trail off the beaten path in a lush, wooded setting offers the challenges that a nature hike brings.**
- **See a beaver dam and catch glimpses of the lagoon from a ridge top.**

TRAILHEAD DIRECTIONS & PARKING:

From Ferry Dock on Main Street turn right. Drive two blocks to Middle Road (note brown sign for Big Bay State Park); turn left. Travel 4 miles to stop sign (road name then changes to Hagen Road). Continue straight for 2 miles and turn left to park office. At first park stop sign turn right toward Campground, Picnic Area and Beach. At next stop sign turn right toward Picnic Area and Beach, then left to Barrier Beach and paved parking lot. Wheelchair accessible parking, moped parking and bike racks available.

TRAILHEAD FACILITIES & FEES:

Vault toilets (wheelchair accessible), water, picnic area (see Barrier Beach Picnic Area, pg. 193). Annual or day use state park permit is required and is available at the park office.

TOTAL TRAIL LENGTH, SURFACE & WIDTH:

2.2 miles; hardpacked dirt; average 1–2' wide. Significant root, minimal rock.

INCLINES & ALERTS:

There are three inclines ranging from 16–22°. Steepest incline is 22° for 10' on return at 2.0 miles. Portions of hike follow ridge top; stay on trail and use caution. Wet and muddy areas prominent in bog. Uneven surfaces throughout entire trail as well as several laid log paths. Overgrowth probable during summer months. Some trees across path at time of writing (August 2003), but easily negotiable. Deer hunting season begins October 15 and hiking on this trail is NOT recommended throughout that season.

CONTACT:

Big Bay State Park: (715) 747-6425

MILEAGE & DESCRIPTION

0.0 Trailhead begins on paved path at north end of parking area toward restrooms. Behind restrooms, walk left through open field toward the blue naturalist shed and fire ring to find sign indicating "Boardwalk to Barrier Beach." Near the sign will be a small box containing free brochures regarding bird, wildflower and fern identification in addition to park maps. The informational kiosk near fire ring also posts schedules of naturalist/environmental programs. Path turns to gravel and hardpacked dirt.

0.1 Continue to follow path and at Y veer left following sign indicating "Campground." In 50' find another trail intersection and locate sign near woods indicating "Lagoon Ridge Trail 2.5 miles." Take this path and soon you will find another sign indicating "Natural Trail with minimum improvements—new trail to park." This serves as a reminder that this hike has a significant amount of root and contains other conditions mentioned in Alert section above.

0.2 Cross bridge (wood, double handrail). Here you will find a decline of 22° for 10', which will be an incline upon return. Soon it will become apparent that you are ascending a ridge that affords nice views of the forest floor beneath. In 200' trail narrows considerably. Short sections of boardwalk begin and continue sporadically throughout the remainder of trail.

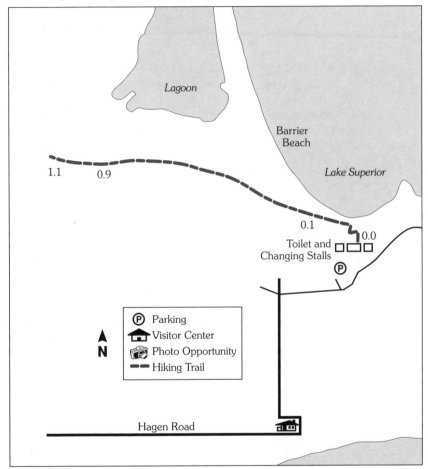

0.3 Cross bridge (wood, double handrail) over a picturesque area.

0.5 Cross bridge. In about 50' look to your left to find the work of nature's lumberjack. Notice the number of trees that were brought down by the beaver's strong front teeth.

0.6 On a clear day views of the lagoon peek through the trees to your right.

0.8   Stands of hemlock on the ridge top provide lovely, filtered shade. Inhale deeply as this is a wonderfully fragrant area. Listen for birds and watch for squirrels and chipmunks in this mixed forest of balsam fir, cedars, birch and maple.

0.9   Look left (about 5' off the trail) through the thimbleberry patch to see a
   unique bench that has been hewn out of a huge fallen tree. Thimbleberry made it inaccessible in summer, but it is still an intriguing sight.

1.0   Notice pink quartz rock right in the middle of the trail. In 200' cross bridge
   (wood, double handrail) and in another 200' look left for yet another unique bench that has been hewn out of a much smaller log. This one is approachable and timely for a break. It is set amidst a stand of birch and overlooks a swampy area.

In another 200' you will be descending the ridge onto a bridge over a swamp. There is an 18° decline for 10' preceding the bridge. Stop on this bridge (wood, double handrail) and look left. Can you locate the beaver dam? We chose this location as a definitive turn-around point to keep within the length criteria set for our book. Trail does continue another 1.5 miles, but to complete this section, turn around on this bridge and retrace path to trailhead.

2.0   Area of steepest incline (22° for 10').

2.2   Trailhead.

🦉 SAYS WHO?

Hiking + soda pop = discomfort!

Soft drinks are not recommended as a fluid replacement because of their concentrated sugars, carbonation, and/or caffeine contents. Carbonation takes up space in the stomach that could be used by additional fluids. And caffeine causes you to lose more fluid than is contained in the drink itself!

Nutrition: Concepts and Controversies [51]

BIG BAY TOWN PARK TRAIL

Madeline Island • Off WI 13, 78 miles from Superior, 20 miles from Ashland

- **Breathtaking views of the crystal clear waters of Big Bay Lagoon.**
- **Spectacular views of Lake Superior.**
- **A magnificent beach area, which is very popular in summer.**

TRAILHEAD DIRECTIONS & PARKING:

From Ferry Dock on Main Street turn left. Follow Main Street around right curve. It will become Big Bay Road and County Road H. At intersection with North Shore Road stay to right on County Road H. Continue past Black's Shanty Road for 2 miles. Follow green sign for Big Bay Town Park. Turn right into Town Park and left to beach parking in sand and gravel lot. Designated wheelchair parking available.

TRAILHEAD FACILITIES & FEES:

Vault toilets (wheelchair accessible), water, picnic area (see Big Bay Town Park Picnic Area pg. 194).

TOTAL TRAIL LENGTH, SURFACE & WIDTH:

0.9 mile; soft sand, hardpacked dirt; trail width difficult to determine because of terrain.

INCLINES & ALERTS:

There are no inclines greater than 10°. Pets are not permitted as this trail is near the beach area. No lifeguard on duty. Soft sand may pose difficulty for some. Although no camping is permitted along any portion of this trail, there are numerous campsites near parking area; please be respectful of campers.

CONTACT:

Madeline Island Chamber of Commerce: (715) 747-2801

MILEAGE & DESCRIPTION

0.0

Trailhead begins at east end of parking lot on 10'-wide sand and gravel path past picnic area. Spectacular views come early at 150' as you find a bench to the far right that provides a stunning overlook of Big Bay Lagoon! The trek down the 33 steps (wood, double handrail, non-continuous) affords closer yet equally stunning views of the lagoon. Find another strategically placed bench en route for additional lagoon view.

Once on bridge (wood, double handrail), pause for a moment. This place is incredibly scenic. To the right lies a wonderful view of the lagoon. To the left is the mouth of the lagoon as it empties into Lake Superior. Straight down on either side of the bridge are the crystal clear waters of Big Bay Lagoon. See how many different species of fish you can identify as visibility may be excellent. Just across the bridge during the summer, canoe rentals are available if you want to paddle the lagoon and give your legs a rest from hiking.

Veer right after canoe outfitter and head between the trees on 10–12'-wide sand and dirt path. En route on this trail you will traverse some soft sand.

0.1 The hiking trail is loosely defined at this point but if you take those paths closest to the beach you will find it. Enjoy the beautiful views of Lake Superior and Big Bay.

0.2 The trail enters a wooded area through a forest of predominately red and white pine.

0.4 Continue on trail until you reach boardwalk. The trail continues for another 1.6 miles into Big Bay State Park (Boardwalk Interpretive Trail pg. 120); to complete this section, turn around and retrace path to trailhead.

0.9 Trailhead.

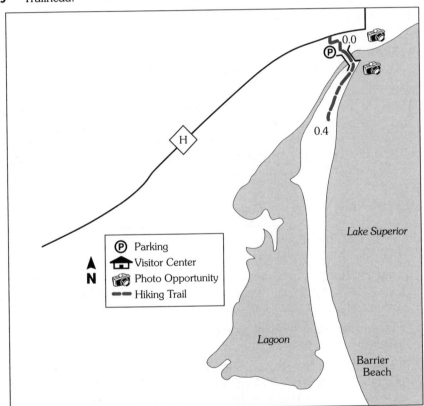

 Foot Note:

Bog Lake Outfitters rents canoes, rowboats and paddleboats on an hourly to daily rate and is on location along this trail (seasonal). For more information call (715) 747-2685.

CASPER TRAIL

Madeline Island • Off WI 13, 78 miles from Superior, 20 miles from Ashland

- **Pushes the boundaries of gentle, but if you seek a solitary trail in a lush wooded setting and are up for the challenge that a minimally maintained trail brings, this one's for you!**

TRAILHEAD DIRECTIONS & PARKING:
From Ferry Dock on Main Street turn left. Follow Main Street around right curve. It will become Big Bay Road and County Road H. Just 0.4 mile from the Ferry Dock find a very small gravel parking area on the right side of the road across from the Emergency Services Building.

TRAILHEAD FACILITIES & FEES:
None.

TOTAL TRAIL LENGTH, SURFACE & WIDTH:
1.8 miles; hardpacked dirt; average 1–2' wide. Significant root, minimal rock.

INCLINES & ALERTS:
There are no inclines greater than 10°. Trailhead may be challenging to locate. Trail is minimally maintained and consequently, at time of writing (August 2003), there were several trees down that required some scrambling to get over, under or around. Trail is very uneven with some laid log paths. Expect wet, muddy areas and overgrowth in summer.

CONTACT:
Madeline Island Chamber of Commerce: (715) 747-2801

MILEAGE & DESCRIPTION

0.0 Trailhead begins off east side of small parking area on narrow trail near sign indicating "Casper Trail." Immediately enter an old growth forest of pine, spruce, cedar, maple, aspen and oak. This densely shaded area delivers a true wilderness feel just yards into the hike!

0.2 Find sign indicating "Wilderness Park Madeline Island Wilderness Preserve." It definitely lives up to its name.

0.3 Intersection with Nucy Meech Trail. Bench here affords views of the forest primeval. Do not take the Meech Trail but continue on Casper Trail. As you walk along notice the logs on the forest floor with lush green moss coverings.

0.5 Find sign indicating "Casper Trail." To the left is another marker indicating Nucy Meech Trail. The Meech Trail was much overgrown. Stay on Casper Trail.

0.9 At trail intersection find tree with hiker icon and arrow pointing left. We recommend turning around at this point and retracing path to trailhead. If you continue left, you will encounter a swampy area and in approximately 150', a small water crossing with no bridge.

1.8 Trailhead.

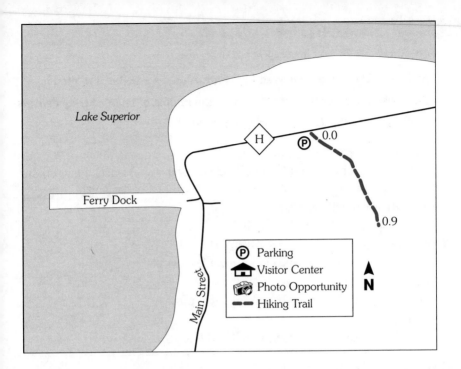

Want to improve your relationship? Take a hike together.

Walking together improves relationships because of the time spent talking without distractions.

Health [38]

IRON BRIDGE AND NATURE TRAIL

Bayfield • Off WI 13, 78 miles from Superior, 20 miles from Ashland

- **An incredibly luscious wooded hike featuring spectacular fern glades.**
- **The "Take me away from it all" trail in the middle of town—it truly delivers!**
- **Walk beneath the 230' Iron Bridge built in 1912.**

TRAILHEAD DIRECTIONS & PARKING:
From WI 13, turn west on County Road I (Washington Avenue). Between 2nd and Broad Streets is a parking area on the north side of the street.

TRAILHEAD FACILITIES & FEES:
No facilities available. No fees for trail use.

TOTAL TRAIL LENGTH, SURFACE & WIDTH:
0.4 mile; gravel, hardpacked dirt; average 2–4' wide.

INCLINES & ALERTS:
There are no inclines over 10°. Overgrowth possible.

CONTACT:
Bayfield Chamber of Commerce: (800) 447-4094

MILEAGE & DESCRIPTION

0.0 Trailhead begins at base of steps near Apple Shed interpretive sign. Take some time to read this sign and explore the landmark. Imagine what it must have been like in its prime. Then ascend 12 steps (wood and dirt, no handrail). At top of hill, turn left and continue to next set of steps. Descend 15 steps (wood and dirt, no handrail).

Enter a spectacular canopy of pines before crossing raised boardwalk (wood, double handrail, benches) with interpretive sign nearby. After boardwalk, encounter small area of erosion. Find another bench and interpretive sign followed by another area of erosion.

0.1 Ascend 1 step (wood and dirt, no handrail) and find the entrance to another raised boardwalk. Descend 4 steps to boardwalk (wood, double handrail) and take some time here to notice the beautiful fern glade beneath the iron bridge. This 230' iron bridge was built in 1912 by Wausau Iron Works to replace the original wooden trestle that served to "bridge" the ravine between two parts of town known as "School Hill" and "Catholic Hill." Several benches are scattered throughout this area for your leisure.

A babbling brook serenades as the valley of ferns decorate this trail. At the intersection on the end of the boardwalk, go left to see the brook up-close on a wooden deck (handrails) with benches to allow a peaceful interlude. Retrace your steps back to the intersection with the boardwalk and go to the left up 11 steps (wood, double handrail) and continue on path. In about 100' ascend another 7 steps (wood, no handrail) to a deck bench. Continue on path and at trail intersection, veer left; this takes you on a scenic trail along the creek bed.

The path to the right just goes up a hill and dead ends shortly after.

0.2 Trail does cross creek bed, but since there is no bridge, we strongly recommend that you turn around here. Though the trail does continue, the steps on the other side of the creek were in serious disrepair and a safety hazard. Trail dead ends shortly after. Retrace path to trailhead.

0.4 Trailhead.

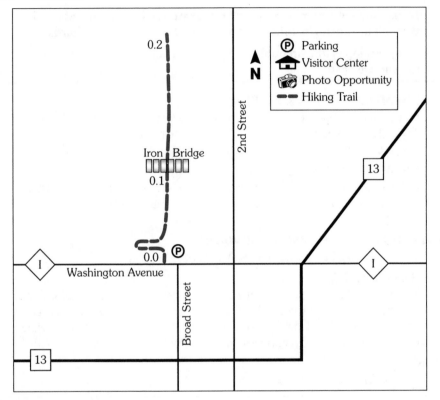

🥾 **Foot Note:**

The Old Iron Bridge is listed on the National Register of Historic Places and is a key structure in the Bayfield Historic District. Although similar to some bridges in the New England area, this style of bridge structure is unique in Wisconsin.

HAUSER ORCHARDS "A-PEELING" STROLL*

Bayfield • Off WI 13, 78 miles from Superior, 20 miles from Ashland • *Gentle Hikes name

- **Your chance to hike through the oldest active orchard in Bayfield, established 1908.**

- **Lovely wooded trail of maple, oak and scattered birch leads into and through a stunning wildflower meadow and active apple orchard.**

- **Enjoy picking your own apples (August/September) or pick a peck from the sample shed.**

TRAILHEAD DIRECTIONS & PARKING:

From WI 13 in Bayfield, turn west on County Road I (Washington Avenue). Travel 1.4 miles to County Road J; turn right and drive 0.6 mile to Hauser Orchards on the left. Parking available in unpaved lot in front of red barn.

TRAILHEAD FACILITIES & FEES:

Gift shop, wine tasting, samples of jams, jellies and salsa, etc., apple tasting (seasonal), field grown perennials, herbs and vegetables (over 250 varieties—seasonal). No fees for trail use.

TOTAL TRAIL LENGTH, SURFACE & WIDTH:

0.8 mile; grass, hardpacked dirt, sand; average 8–10' wide.

INCLINES & ALERTS:

There are no inclines greater than 10°. Owner grants public access through private property. Please be respectful. Must cross farm road—watch for working vehicles. At time of writing, trail through wooded section had just been created resulting in rough and uneven terrain in places. Moderate root and rock in first half of trail.

CONTACT:

Bayfield Winery LTD: (715) 779-5404

MILEAGE & DESCRIPTION

0.0 Trailhead begins beyond north side of the parking lot (past the red Sears and Roebuck barn) at sign near entrance to woods. At time of writing, trail through wooded section was about 6' wide and marked with orange ties and wooden signs. Alert: This new wooded section of trail has rough and uneven sections with moderate root, rock and small stumps.

Trail quickly enters a lovely, shaded forest of maple and oak with a few birch and pine scattered throughout. This woodland area can afford many photo opportunities depending upon the sunlight filtering through the trees.

0.1 At intersection, follow sign to right called Woodpecker Trail.

0.2 At next trail intersection, turn left at sign for Wildflower Trail. Path leads to another intersection where you will take a right at another sign marking the Wildflower Trail.

0.3 Turn left at next intersection at sign stating Wildflower South Trail and hike out of wooded area. Stay on grassy path that leads straight ahead (do NOT veer left toward barn area). Depending upon season, this section of trail leads through a beautiful meadow filled with colorful and fragrant wildflowers. If you are visiting during summer, you will be able to experience the sight and fragrance of over 20 acres of wildflowers! Bring the camera. This is simply gorgeous.

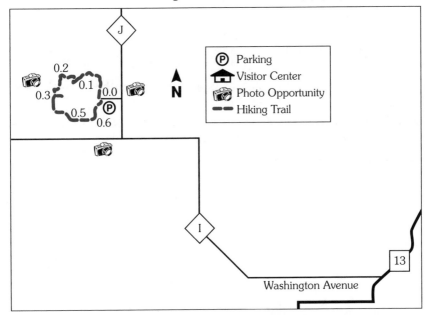

0.4 Follow path to left past a line of old Norway spruce and into the orchard area. Trail opens wider; you will cross a farm road (remember this is a working farm—watch for vehicles). Continue through the orchard.

0.6 The last part of trail is a sandy path leading toward a grassy area. On a clear day views of Madeline Island and the Porcupine Mountains of Michigan may be visible from this hilltop. The small red building is Grandma Hauser's kitchen where she prepares her homemade jams and jellies. You will find samples available in the big red Sears and Roebuck barn near the parking area.

0.7 Continue on grass around back side of the house, staying to the right of clothesline and red shed. Yes, this is private property, but owner grants public access through it. Please be respectful. Follow sidewalk past Hauser's und Haus.

Don't leave before taking the Almost Hike (Hauser's Superior View pg. 166) for a great view from the top of the 1920s Sears and Roebuck barn. Afterward, enjoy some samples of the various goods produced at this farm. Don't be surprised if you're greeted by one of the friendly orchard dogs who will beg you to stay just a little longer.

0.8 This completes a loop and returns you to the parking area and trailhead.

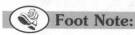 **Foot Note:**

Bayfield is home to many orchards, berry farms and commercial flower farms where visitors are encouraged to pick pails of apples, raspberries, strawberries, cherries and blueberries. For more information, pick up a Bayfield Visitor Guide or contact the Bayfield Chamber of Commerce (800-447-4094 or www.bayfield.org).

 SAYS WHO?

An apple a day keeps more than just the doctor away—it may keep heart disease, cancer, stroke, diabetes and asthma at bay!

A recent Finnish study on over 10,000 people found that apple eaters have a lower risk of heart disease, cancer, stroke, type 2 diabetes and asthma.

American Journal of Clinical Nutrition [52]

BROWNSTONE TRAIL NORTH

Bayfield • Off WI 13, 79 miles from Superior, 19 miles from Ashland

• Lovely, flat trail affords scenic views of Lake Superior.

TRAILHEAD DIRECTIONS & PARKING:
From WI 13, turn east on Manypenny Avenue to 3rd Street. Turn right on 3rd and park in paved lot at Department of Natural Resources building.

TRAILHEAD FACILITIES & FEES:
No facilities available. No fees for trail use.

TOTAL TRAIL LENGTH, SURFACE & WIDTH:
0.9 mile; gravel, hardpacked dirt; average 4–8' wide.

INCLINES & ALERTS:
There are no inclines greater than 10°. There were two areas of erosion on this trail at time of writing (June 2003).

CONTACT:
Bayfield Chamber of Commerce: (800) 447-4094

MILEAGE & DESCRIPTION

0.0 Trailhead may be challenging to locate. You must walk through the lumber yard to reach the two-track path leading into a wooded area. Shortly the trail changes to a single path as it travels through a densely wooded area.

0.1 Scenic views of Lake Superior can be seen throughout the remainder of this trail.

0.3 This section contains an uneven area of erosion.

0.4 This trail does continue (see Brownstone Trail South, pg. 140); however, at the time of writing there was a fence indicating end of trail due to some very major erosion. Do not bypass the fence as there is a much easier and safer access point on Brownstone Trail South. Turn around and retrace path to trailhead.

0.9 Trailhead.

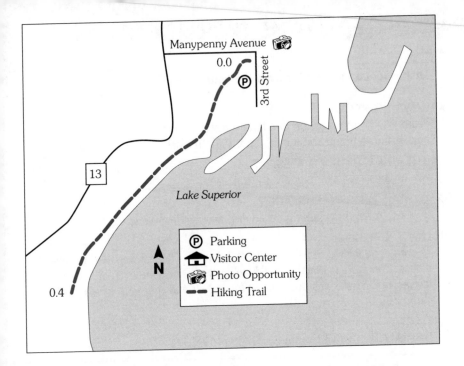

At risk for developing diabetes?

Studies showed that for every 2000 calories spent in leisure activities, diabetes was reduced by 24%.

Exercise and Sports Science Reviews [2]

BROWNSTONE TRAIL SOUTH

Bayfield • Off WI 13, 81 miles from Superior, 17 miles from Ashland

---

- **Lush wooded hike not far from the heart of Bayfield.**

TRAILHEAD DIRECTIONS & PARKING:
From WI 13, turn east on Sanitarium Road. At first Y in road, turn right; at next Y turn left and continue to end. Park in small paved cul-de-sac.

TRAILHEAD FACILITIES & FEES:
No facilities available. No fees for trail use.

TOTAL TRAIL LENGTH, SURFACE & WIDTH:
2 miles; grass, gravel, hardpacked dirt; average 4–8' wide.

INCLINES & ALERTS:
There is one incline of 12° for 20' at 1.1 mile. Trail crosses road in several places. Some areas may be muddy when wet. Trail is uneven at beginning due to washout. There was one area of erosion at end of trail at time of writing (June 2003).

CONTACT:
Bayfield Chamber of Commerce: (800) 447-4094

MILEAGE & DESCRIPTION

0.0 Trailhead begins at end of cul-de-sac at sign indicating "Brownstone Trail." Enter into a lush canopy of birch and maple. Numerous spurs lead to private property—please be courteous and stay on trail. At time of writing, this section was uneven and wet due to washout from heavy rains.

0.1 Spur to the left goes to Wild Rice Restaurant. Depending on foliage throughout this trail you may be treated to glimpses of beautiful Lake Superior.

0.3 When first house comes into view, look left for a section of steps leading up the hill; at time of writing there was no sign. Although the trail continues straight ahead, due to private property it has been rerouted. Ascend 24 steps (wood and gravel, no handrail, non-continuous). Continue on this rerouting of trail as it passes behind private property.

0.5 Alert: Trail crosses Blue Wing Bay Road—use caution.

0.6 At interpretive marker turn right and travel downhill to rejoin main trail. Turn left at trail intersection.

0.8 Alert: Trail crosses Lakeshore Drive—use caution.

0.9 Alert: Trail crosses driveway behind garage—use caution.

1.0 This trail does continue (see Brownstone Trail North, pg. 138); however, at the time of writing, there was a fence indicating end of trail due to some very major erosion. Do not bypass the fence as there is a much easier and safer access point on Brownstone Trail North. Turn around and retrace path to trailhead.

1.1 Area of steepest incline (12° for 20').

2.0 Trailhead.

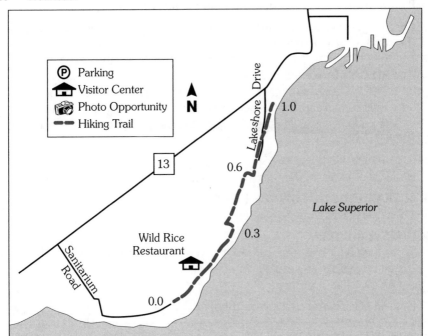

 SAYS WHO?

Want to curb your appetite? Get out and take in the sights!

Walking has been shown to induce a short term reduction of appetite in most people.

Circulation [18]

WASHBURN WALKING TRAIL

Washburn • Off WI 13, 91 miles from Superior, 7 miles from Ashland

- **Beautiful views of Lake Superior's Chequamegon Bay.**
- **Catch a glimpse of the spectacular sandy cliffs that are the signature of the south shore of Lake Superior.**

TRAILHEAD DIRECTIONS & PARKING:

From WI 13, turn south on Washington Avenue toward Lake Superior. You will drive only 0.2 mile to find a small gravel and grass parking area, which itself provides a lovely view of Chequamegon Bay. Designated wheelchair accessible parking available.

TRAILHEAD FACILITIES & FEES:

No facilities available. No fees for trail use.

TOTAL TRAIL LENGTH, SURFACE & WIDTH:

1.9 miles; gravel; average 6' wide.

INCLINES & ALERTS:

There are no inclines over 10°. Path travels through marina area, which is shared by vehicles and equipment—use caution.

CONTACT:

Bayfield Chamber of Commerce: (800) 447-4094

MILEAGE & DESCRIPTION

0.0 Trailhead begins on 6'-wide gravel path at sign stating No Motorized Vehicles Allowed. At trail intersection, turn left (trail continues to the right as well (see Washburn Walking Trail Wheelchair Accessible Section pg. 144). Take some time to read about Washburn's past on the large interpretive sign. Descend 22 steps (wood and gravel, no handrail, non-continuous); cross bridge (wood, double handrail). At the end of bridge is access to a lovely beach area where photo ops abound. Turn left and ascend 8 uneven steps (wood, handrail).

0.1 This sections offers continuous lovely views of Lake Superior's Chequamegon Bay.

0.2 Descend 6 steps (wood and gravel, no handrail), cross bridge (wood, double handrail), then descend 4 additional steps (wood, no handrail). Please respect private property as there are homes in this area.

0.3 Spur to fishing pier and view of marina. Stay on main trail. Shortly, descend 8 steps (wood, no handrail), cross bridge (wood, double handrail), then descend 2 steps (wood, double handrail).

0.4 Alert: You are now entering marina area, which is shared by vehicles and equipment—use caution. Cross boat launch to boardwalk.

0.5 At end of boardwalk, turn left crossing pavement to walk along pier (no guardrail). Trail is very loosely defined at this point.

0.6 Continue to end of pier where gravel trail becomes evident; turn left. Views of the shoreline become visible. See if you can catch a glimpse of the spectacular sandy cliffs, which are the signature of the south shore of Lake Superior. Cross road to pick up gravel trail on other side. You will find a spur trail to the beach area.

0.8 Two benches afford wonderful views of the Ashland shoreline across Chequamegon Bay.

0.9 This section of trail closely parallels a road that is used by vehicles and ATVs. Soon this section of the Washburn Walking Trail ends. Turn around and retrace path to trailhead.

1.9 Trailhead.

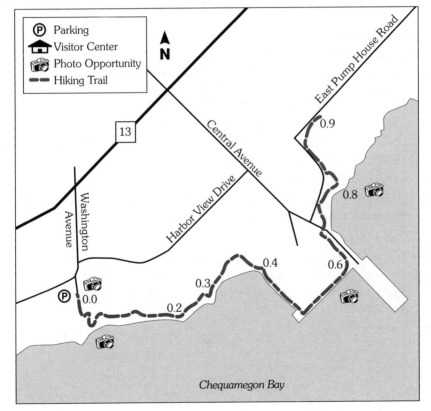

WASHBURN WALKING TRAIL (WHEELCHAIR ACCESSIBLE SECTION)

Washburn • Off WI 13, 91 miles from Superior, 7 miles from Ashland

- **Beautiful views of Lake Superior's Chequamegon Bay.**

TRAILHEAD DIRECTIONS & PARKING:
From WI 13, turn south on 6th Avenue W toward Lake Superior. Drive just 0.2 mile to paved parking lot. This is also the boat launch area—use caution.

TRAILHEAD FACILITIES & FEES:
No facilities available. No fees for trail use.

TOTAL TRAIL LENGTH, SURFACE & WIDTH:
0.8 mile; gravel; average 6' wide.

INCLINES & ALERTS:
There are no inclines over 10°. You may need to pass through the boat launch area to access trailhead.

CONTACT:
Bayfield Chamber of Commerce: (800) 447-4094

MILEAGE & DESCRIPTION

0.0 Trailhead begins at sign indicating Walking Trail on 6'-wide gravel path. Soon you will see two rather large informational boards to the left. Take some time to read about Washburn's lumber days. Enjoy views of Lake Superior's Chequamegon Bay as you continue along the trail.

0.1 Cross bridge (wood, double handrail). Continue past picnic table and on to upper portion of the trail where views of Ashland's breakwater lighthouse can be seen in the far distance.

0.2 Cross quaint iron railed bridge.

0.3 A strategically placed bench may afford birding opportunities and provides nice views of Chequamegon Bay.

0.4 Another bench provides views of the marina. Shortly, the wheelchair accessible section of this trail ends. Trail continues (see Washburn Walking Trail pg. 142), but to complete this section of the trail, turn around and retrace path to trailhead.

0.8 Trailhead.

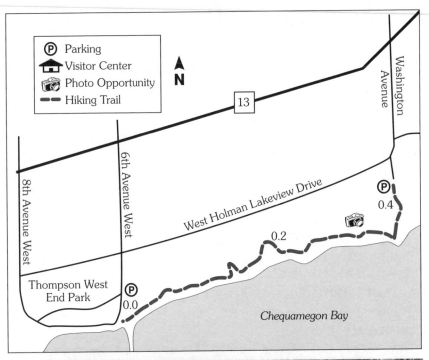

Bridge along the Washburn Walking Trail (Wheelchair Accessible Section). Photo by Melanie Morgan

LONG LAKE TRAIL

Chequamegon-Nicolet National Forest • Off WI 13, 93 miles from Superior, 5 miles from Ashland

- **An incredibly beautiful wooded trail with spectacular views of Long Lake.**
- **Long boardwalk opens marsh for close-up viewing.**

TRAILHEAD DIRECTIONS & PARKING:

From WI 13 south of Washburn turn west on Wanabo Road (various spellings, e.g., Wannebo, Wanabo, Wanebo). Travel 6 miles to sign for Chequamegon National Forest Picnic Grounds, Long Lake; turn right. Drive 0.1 mile to sign for Long Lake picnic grounds, boat landing; turn left and continue to paved parking area. Ample parking available with designated wheelchair accessible parking.

TRAILHEAD FACILITIES & FEES:

Vault toilets (wheelchair accessible), water, picnic area (see Long Lake Picnic Area pg. 196), beach (no lifeguard). U.S. Forest vehicle stickers are required to park in this lot or day use fee of $3 (self-pay).

TOTAL TRAIL LENGTH, SURFACE & WIDTH:

1.7 miles; pavement, hardpacked dirt; average 1–2' wide. Minimal rock and root.

INCLINES & ALERTS:

There are no inclines greater than 10°. Overgrowth throughout the trail may be problematic in summer. Steep cliffs on ridge section above lake. Boardwalk may be damaged or uneven in sections.

CONTACT:

Chequamegon-Nicolet National Forest (Washburn Office): (715) 373-2667

MILEAGE & DESCRIPTION

0.0 Trailhead begins on pavement at kiosk near pump off northwest corner of parking lot. Continue right into woods at end of pavement on hardpacked dirt path. This is simply a gorgeous wooded hike.

0.1 At Y in trail, turn left. In this section you will encounter a bench that provides a wonderful photo op of Long Lake.

0.6 Open area for carry-in boat launch. Parking is also available near this location. Benches afford more opportunities for observing waterfowl and taking photos.

0.7 At next Y, spur to left leads to lake; continue to right. In approximately 700' encounter boardwalk over marsh. Alert: Boardwalk may be damaged or uneven in sections. This area offers spectacular views of Long Lake as well as a glimpse of a beaver lodge.

0.9 Ascend 4 steps (wood and hardpacked dirt, no handrail) to a bench that provides yet another photo op of the marsh.

1.1 Cross narrow bridge (wood, no handrail).

1.2 Notice that the trail follows a small, narrow ridge through the forest in this section. Alert: Steep cliffs on ridge section above lake.

1.5 At Y in trail, turn left. Be observant of uneven pavement as you enter beach area. Ascend 12 steps (concrete, double handrail, non-continuous) to picnic area.

1.6 Pavement begins at top of steps. Return to trailhead via picnic area.

1.7 Trailhead.

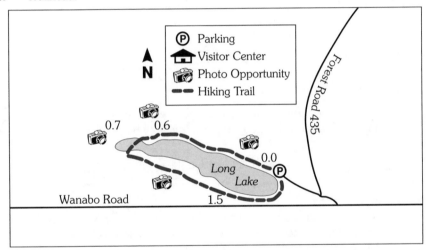

TWIN LAKES TRAIL

Birch Grove Campground, Chequamegon-Nicolet National Forest • Off WI 13, 93 miles from Superior, 5 miles from Ashland

- **This trail provides a wonderful wilderness experience.**
- **Wide variety of ferns in spring and summer with some of surprising height.**

TRAILHEAD DIRECTIONS & PARKING:

From WI 13 south of Washburn turn west on Wanabo Road (various spellings, e.g., Wannebo, Wanabo, Wanebo). Travel 6 miles to sign for Chequamegon National Forest picnic grounds, Long Lake; turn right. Stay on Forest Road 435 and travel 2.9 miles to sign for Birch Grove Campground; turn left. Drive 0.1 mile to gravel parking lot on right side of road.

TRAILHEAD FACILITIES & FEES:

Vault toilets and water nearby, small picnic area with grill, boat launch, campground. No fees for trail use.

TOTAL TRAIL LENGTH, SURFACE & WIDTH:

1 mile; hardpacked dirt; average 1' wide. Minimal rock and root.

INCLINES & ALERTS:

There are no inclines greater than 10°. Final tenth of trail follows entrance road to parking lot. Overgrowth throughout the trail may be problematic in summer.

CONTACT:

Chequamegon-Nicolet National Forest (Washburn Office): (715) 373-2667

MILEAGE & DESCRIPTION

0.0   Trailhead begins at southwest corner of parking area by boat launch. Begin your journey by following the trail beside the lake into a beautiful, heavily wooded area. Spur trails to the left lead to campsites; please be courteous and respectful. Trails to the right lead to lake.

0.1   Trail meanders away from lake and takes you into a forest of red and white pine, oak, birch, maple and a variety of ferns.

0.5   Spur trail to the left (boardwalk visible) leads to interpretive area that was under construction at time of writing (June 2003).

0.7   Trail turns closer to the lake; look directly across to see the parking area from which you began this hike.

0.8   Spur to the right leads to a point of land that juts out into the lake.

0.9   This concludes the trail. Turn right and follow entrance road to parking area and trailhead.

1.0   Trailhead.

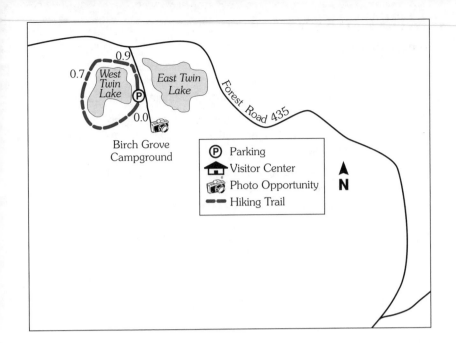

Do you have high blood pressure?

Physical activity such as walking can help to reduce and prevent high blood pressure.

Preventive Medicine [48]

ALMOST HIKES

An Almost Hike is:

-a very short trail, ranging from 90' to 0.4 mile with spectacular scenery.
-typically not a trail per se, but a route to scenic beauty.
-usually has an original name as this concept is original to our book.

We hope you'll enjoy the following strolls. We give you highlights, total length/surface, safety concerns, amenities, applicable fees and a brief narrative of what you'll see while there.

Most Almost Hikes are very suitable for families travelling with small children. Great leg stretchers and highly scenic—but please heed safety concerns.

Wisconsin Point Lighthouse (pg. 153). Photo by Ladona Tornabene

RHONDA & JOE'S WEDDING STROLL*

Superior • Off U.S. 2, 4 miles from Superior-Douglas County Visitor Center • *Gentle Hikes name

- **Incredible overlook of St. Louis Bay.**
- **Nice stroll through main features of Billings Park.**

DIRECTIONS & PARKING:
From the Superior-Douglas County Visitor Center head east on U.S. 2 for 1.7 miles. At Tower Ave (WI 35) turn left (south) and travel 0.5 mile to 21st Street. Turn right (west) and travel 1.6 miles to sign for Billings Park; drive around traffic circle to Billings Drive. Turn right and continue to next Billings Park sign and arrow pointing to the right. Turn here and drive to small paved lot at end of in-drive. Parking is also allowed on one side of drive—please note signs.

TRAILHEAD FACILITIES & FEES:
Flush toilets (wheelchair accessible), water spigot, picnic area (see Billings Park Picnic Area pg. 185). No fees for trail use.

TOTAL LENGTH/SURFACE:
0.4 miles; paved, ending in open grassy area.

ALERT:
Pavement uneven in places.

NARRATIVE:
Trailhead begins from the right of parking lot on 4'-wide paved path, which runs parallel to park road and through the main features of Billings Park, including some small but pretty garden areas. You will pass the pavilion, volleyball court and horseshoe pits, a playground and another very unique playground designed specifically for those with disabilities. The steps located at the far edge of this unique playground lead to the Riverfront Trail (see pg. 28). Continue to follow paved path through more picnic areas until it ends at the park entrance. Turn around and retrace path to trailhead. Once at trailhead, continue onto the large grassy area that sports a swing and bench with fabulous views of the St. Louis Bay—not to be missed. Friends of the authors had an outdoor wedding here and bride and groom as well as many guests walked this Almost Hike!

WELCOME-A-BOARD-WALK*

Superior • Off U.S. 2, 0.1 mile from Superior-Douglas County Visitor Center • *Gentle Hikes name

- **Enter the world's only remaining whaleback ship built in Superior in 1896.**

- **Browse numerous gift shops or challenge the family to a game of mini golf.**

- **Enjoy lovely views of Superior Bay.**

DIRECTIONS & PARKING:

From U.S. 2 at the Superior-Douglas County Visitor Center turn east onto service road beside Visitor Center and Bong WWII Heritage Center. Follow signs indicating Barker's Island. Continue to paved parking area near SS Meteor. Designated RV and wheelchair accessible spaces.

TRAILHEAD FACILITIES & FEES:

Flush toilets (located in the SS Meteor but has same hours as gift shops), portable toilet (wheelchair accessible), water fountain, playground—all located off main parking lot. Picnic area (see Barker's Island Play Area Picnic Area pg. 184); each table has a grill. There is a small beach (no lifeguard) near last picnic area. No fees for picnic use. No fees for trail use.

TOTAL LENGTH/SURFACE:

800'; boardwalk.

ALERT:

Boardwalk uneven in places. At time of writing (August 2003), plans were underway to renovate this area but no definite timeframe was given. Therefore if the following description has changed, at least you'll know that we weren't "out to sea" when we wrote it.

NARRATIVE:

Trailhead begins from the west of parking lot on 8'-wide boardwalk, which makes a loop around many of the festivities housed on this end of Barker's Island. Spend some time cruising around the wharf shops and stroll the length of the SS Meteor on the boardwalk, which is literally within arm's reach of the ship. This land-based ship is impressive considering it is the last whaleback remaining of the 44 built. All but four of these whalebacks were constructed in Superior and Duluth. She is 384' long and 45' wide. Nearby is a sailor theme mini golf course, gift shops, eateries, retired boats, bell and even a ship-shaped playground to keep the kids "ship-shape." Strategically placed benches afford lovely views of Superior Bay with the City of Duluth serving as a nice backdrop. Bring the camera because there will be a lot of smiles!

 Foot Note:

Tour the SS Meteor and Maritime Museum (seasonal) and see the last remaining whaleback ship. For more information call (715) 392-5742 or visit www.ssmeteor.org.

WISCONSIN POINT LIGHTHOUSE*

Superior • On U.S. 2, 5 miles from Superior-Douglas County Visitor Center, 95 miles from Hurley
*Gentle Hikes name

- **This Almost Hike comes with the added bonus of a scenic drive past Allouez Bay then through a forest canopy of pines with numerous beach access points.**

- **Commanding view of picturesque Wisconsin Point Lighthouse.**
- **Spectacular views of Lake Superior's sandy beach shoreline.**

DIRECTIONS & PARKING:
On U.S. 2 at the point where the highway splits and becomes a divided four lane, turn north on Moccasin Mike Road. Follow for 1.5 miles and look for brown sign with binocular icon. (Note: if you passed the landfill, you went too far.) Turn left onto paved road just beyond brown sign and travel 3 miles past several pull-outs to beach areas. If you have the time, pull over and take some of the walk-outs to get different views of this beautiful Superior sandy shoreline! After passing the Chippewa burial site, take the next right onto a gravel road. Soon you will see the lighthouse. Park in gravel lot.

AMENITIES & FEES:
None.

TOTAL LENGTH/SURFACE:
710', cement.

ALERT:
No 4-wheelers or snowmobiles allowed. Irregular and broken concrete surface. No guardrails. When exploring beach area please stay on sand due to sensitive vegetation.

NARRATIVE:
Trail begins with a step up from the sandy surface onto the 6'-wide concrete pier and ends where the boulders begin. For your safety, do not walk on these uneven boulders that lead to the lighthouse itself. This area affords plenty of scenic beauty with sweeping views of Superior's sandy shoreline. The lighthouse is picturesque in its own right, but looks stunning when framed by the rocks in the foreground. Venture onto the beach area for some creative photo ops! Before you leave, visit the Superior Entry Almost Hike (pg. 154), which is right around the corner.

 Foot Note:

"As I travel, I hope I leave beautiful footsteps behind me." Bill Brunette, Chairman, S.I.O. 1985.

SUPERIOR ENTRY
Superior • On U.S. 2, 5 miles from Superior-Douglas County Visitor Center, 95 miles from Hurley

- **Of historical significance: This is the only natural opening through the longest freshwater sandbar in the world!**

DIRECTIONS & PARKING:
On U.S. 2 at the point where the highway splits and becomes a divided four lane, turn north on Moccasin Mike Road. Follow for 1.5 miles and look for

brown sign with binocular icon. (Note: if you passed the landfill, you went too far.) Turn left onto paved road just beyond brown sign and travel 3 miles past several pull-outs to beach areas. If you have the time, pull over and take some of the walk-outs to get different views of this beautiful Superior sandy shoreline! After passing the Chippewa burial site, you will eventually come to a Y in the road as the paved portion ends. Turn right (you cannot go to the left as it is a posted area with no trespassing sign) and park in gravel lot.

AMENITIES & FEES:
None.

TOTAL LENGTH/SURFACE:
0.3 miles; cement.

ALERT:
Very uneven paved section just prior to 30' cement pier.

NARRATIVE:
Trailhead begins at 4'-wide sidewalk, which leads to the 30'-wide pier near sign indicating 'The Superior Entry'. Before beginning this Almost Hike, take time to read about the history of this opening, which was first chartered in 1861. As you stroll out to the end of the sidewalk, turn right. At time of writing (October, 2003) there was a gouge in the pavement here. In just a few more steps, a small ramp brings you onto the cement pier. This is an interesting location to watch freighters, salties and various small boats as they pass through the Superior port. This is the western terminus of the St. Lawrence Seaway and one of the busiest ports in the United States. Before you leave, visit the Wisconsin Point Lighthouse Almost Hike (pg. 153) that you just passed en route to this location.

BIG MANITOU FALLS

Pattison State Park • Off U.S. 2, 13 miles south of Superior

- **See the highest waterfall in Wisconsin, which plummets 165'!**
- **This location offers the best view of the entire falls—popular photo op.**
- **Lovely wooded picnic area on site.**

DIRECTIONS & PARKING:
From the Superior-Douglas County Visitor Center head west on U.S. 2 for 1.7 miles. Turn left (south) on WI 35 (Tower Ave) and travel 13 miles. Drive 0.1 mile past sign for Pattison State Park. Turn right onto County Road B and almost immediately turn left into paved parking lot. Designed wheelchair accessible parking available.

AMENITIES & FEES:
Vault toilets, grills. Annual or day use state park permit is required and is available at the park office.

TOTAL LENGTH/SURFACE:
0.1 mile; paved, but uneven surface and not flat.

ALERT:
Use caution when crossing County Road B. Steep cliffs near falls (rock wall serves as guardrail).

NARRATIVE:
Trailhead begins on paved path leading out of parking area. Use caution when crossing County Road B. Pick up trail by sign indicating Pedestrian Crossing.

This path splits immediately. Trail to the left is a wheelchair accessible route (but uneven in places due to tree root protrusions) and circles the picnic area. Stay on path straight ahead for a stunning, full-length view of Big Manitou Falls!

This view of the falls can also be reached from a different parking lot to avoid road crossing, but the trail is longer (see Big Manitou Falls Geology Walk pg. 44).

 Foot Note:

The Black River, after plummeting down Big Manitou Falls, flows some 15 miles toward its final destination—Lake Superior. This is just one of the 200 rivers that flow into the greatest of the Great Lakes. Source: State Park Visitor

LITTLE MANITOU FALLS

Pattison State Park • Off U.S. 2, 14 miles south of Superior.

- **Striking views of Little Manitou Falls.**

DIRECTIONS & PARKING:
From the Superior-Douglas County Visitor Center head west on U.S. 2 for 1.7 miles. Turn left (south) on WI 35 (Tower Ave) and travel 13 miles. Watch for sign for Pattison State Park. Continue on WI 35 for 1 additional mile south of main entrance to Pattison State Park. Follow sign and turn left to paved parking areas. Lower lot has designated RV and wheelchair accessible parking. Upper lot for overflow parking or access to canoe pullout.

TOTAL LENGTH & SURFACE:
Approximately 200'; paved.

ALERT:
You will need to cross entrance road to locate trailhead. Steep cliffs with no guardrail. Uneven asphalt.

AMENITIES & FEES:
Vault toilets, water and picnic area nearby (see Pattison State Park Main Picnic Area pg. 186). Annual or day use state park permit is required and available at park office.

NARRATIVE:
Trailhead begins across the entrance road from the parking area. Enter on asphalt surface and descend 7 steps (wood, handrail). Immediately you will hear the

sounds of Little Manitou Falls as it comes into view. Bench to the left for spectacular falls viewing. A little further along the trail affords an even better view. This trail does continue as it is part of the Little Falls Hiking Trail (pg. 54); however, to complete this Almost Hike, turn around here and retrace path to trailhead.

Little Manitou Falls at Pattison State Park. Photo by Ladona Tornabene

AMNICON FALLS WOODED AND RIVERVIEW STROLL*

Amnicon Falls State Park • Off U.S. 2, 12 miles from Superior, 87 miles from Hurley • *Gentle Hikes name

- **Lovely wooded hike with splendid river views.**

DIRECTIONS & PARKING:
On U.S. 2, turn north on County Road U for 0.3 mile; turn left at sign for Amnicon Falls State Park. From office parking area turn left at stop sign, then right and over bridge, following signs for Campground and Nature Trail. Drive 0.2 mile to second small paved parking area on right, beyond open-sided shelter. RV parking is available here or at first paved lot 0.1 mile back.

AMENITIES & FEES:
Vault toilet (wheelchair accessible), water nearby, tables, grill. Annual or day use state park permit is required and available at park office.

TOTAL LENGTH/SURFACE:
0.2 mile; pavement, hardpacked dirt, grass.

ALERT:
Overgrowth possible during summer months.

NARRATIVE:
Trailhead begins at end of pavement opposite wheelchair accessible picnic table. Shortly you will find a bench at trail intersection; turn right. This wide path leads through a beautifully wooded area and into another picnic area. At this point, turn left near the water fountain and pick up the return trail. This section of trail parallels the Amnicon River and offers lovely views. Continue on to trailhead. This trail is part of the Amnicon Falls Picnic Stroll (see pg. 60).

BRULE RIVER VIEW*

Brule • On U.S. 2, 28 miles from Superior, 72 miles from Hurley • *Gentle Hikes name

- **Historical marker about the Brule River.**
- **Picturesque river views.**

DIRECTIONS & PARKING:
On U.S. 2 in Brule, locate lovely wayside on south side of highway. Paved parking available with designated wheelchair accessible and RV spaces.

AMENITIES & FEES:
Vault toilets (wheelchair accessible), water, picnic tables, grills, map kiosk. No fees for trail use.

TOTAL LENGTH/SURFACE:
0.2 mile; paved.

ALERT:
Uneven pavement.

NARRATIVE:
Trailhead begins from west end of parking lot on paved path. Stop to read a little about the history of Daniel Greysolon, Sieur Du Lhut and history of the Brule River. Then take this short stroll out past the artesian well and ascend one step onto the bridge (wood, double handrail). Continue to the picturesque iron bridge that overlooks the point where the Brule and Little Brule meet.

NORTHERN GREAT LAKES VISITOR CENTER INDOOR OUTING*

Northern Great Lakes Visitor Center • On U.S. 2, 60 miles from Superior, 40 miles from Hurley
*Gentle Hikes name

- **Panoramic views of Lake Superior and the Apostle Islands can be seen on a clear day.**
- **A destination unto itself, and all facilities are wheelchair accessible.**

DIRECTIONS & PARKING:
From U.S. 2, turn west at County Road G and sign for Northern Great Lakes Visitor Center. Turn right into paved lot. Ample parking available in paved lot with designated RV and wheelchair accessible parking.

AMENITIES & FEES:
Flush toilets (wheelchair accessible), water, gift shop, 9-county historical archives research center, educational programs, outstanding state-of-the-art exhibit hall, Intriguing Objects Theatre and interactive exhibits. No fees for use.

TOTAL LENGTH/SURFACE:
78 steps, non-continuous. Due to the indoor nature of this Almost Hike, total length and surface are not reported in traditional fashion. Entire facility is barrier-free (see pg. 208 for additional information).

ALERT:
None at time of writing.

NARRATIVE:
We broke format with this one, but we think it delivers—big time! "Trailhead" is located inside Visitor Center at stairs. Ascend 22 steps (double handrail, non-continuous) to 2nd Floor. There you will find displays that pertain to winter travel on Lake Superior as well as artifacts and pictures. Plan to spend some time here before ascending the remaining 56 steps (double handrail, non-continuous) to the Mezzanine Level. Weather permitting, walk out to the Observation Deck. From this vantage point there are magnificent panoramic views of Lake Superior and the Apostle Islands. The trails you see below are the Boardwalk Trail East Loop (pg. 72) and Boardwalk Trail West Loop (pg. 74). Step back inside and enjoy the several interactive displays.

PRENTICE PARK WOODED STROLL*

Prentice Park, Ashland • Off U.S. 2, 62 miles from Superior, 38 miles from Hurley • *Gentle Hikes name

---

• **Simply a lovely path through the woods.**

DIRECTIONS & PARKING:

From U.S. 2 in the west end of Ashland, watch for large brown sign indicating City of Ashland Prentice Park. This can be found near Maslowski Beach. Turn south at sign on Turner Road and drive 0.2 mile to next sign. Turn right and pass picnic pavilion and first right turn down hill. Another right turn follows the RV camping pull-through. At the end of the drive is a small paved parking area.

AMENITIES & FEES:

Picnic tables, grills and BBQ pit. No fees for trail use.

TOTAL LENGTH/SURFACE:

0.2 mile; hardpacked dirt, avg. 2–3' wide.

ALERT:

At time of writing (summer 2003) we were told that plans were being discussed to remove the deer from the deer yard.

NARRATIVE:

Trailhead begins from parking area at chain barricade opposite deer yard and continues through a splendid wooded area to the turn-around point at the park road (also marked by wooden posts). After hiking, plan to spend some time at the deer yard, which is the fenced-in area. Other wildlife has been spotted there also.

PRENTICE PARK PROMENADE (EAST)*

Prentice Park, Ashland • Off U.S. 2, 62 miles from Superior, 38 miles from Hurley • *Gentle Hikes name

---

• **Another gentle, flat, wooded hike through the middle of a lovely park.**

DIRECTIONS & PARKING:

From U.S. 2 in the west end of Ashland, watch for large brown sign indicating City of Ashland Prentice Park. This can be found near Maslowski Beach. Turn south at sign on Turner Road and drive 0.2 mile to next sign. Turn right and continue to paved parking area near picnic pavilion. Designated RV and wheelchair accessible parking.

AMENITIES & FEES:

Flush toilets (wheelchair accessible), water, picnic area (see Prentice Park Picnic Area pg. 189). No fees for trail use.

TOTAL LENGTH/SURFACE:

0.3 mile; grass.

ALERT:

Multi-use trail. No ATVs.

NARRATIVE:

Trailhead begins from east end of parking lot near the women's restroom and continues until the turn-around point where the trail meets Turner Road. This section is nice and wide (approximately 20') with a wooded yet open-sky feel. Look for the nice stand of aspen to the right shortly after starting on the trail.

PRENTICE PARK PROMENADE (WEST)*

Prentice Park, Ashland • Off U.S. 2, 62 miles from Superior, 38 miles from Hurley • *Gentle Hikes name

- **A gentle, flat, wooded hike through the middle of a lovely park.**

DIRECTIONS & PARKING:

From U.S. 2 in the west end of Ashland, watch for large brown sign indicating City of Ashland Prentice Park. This can be found near Maslowski Beach. Turn south at sign on Turner Road and drive 0.2 mile to next sign. Turn right and continue to paved parking area near picnic pavilion. Designated RV and wheelchair accessible parking.

AMENITIES & FEES:

Flush toilets (wheelchair accessible), water, picnic area (see Prentice Park Picnic Area pg. 189). No fees for trail use.

TOTAL LENGTH/SURFACE:

0.2 mile; grass, gravel, dirt.

ALERT:

Multi-use trail. No ATVs.

NARRATIVE:

Trailhead begins from west end of parking lot between road and playground area and runs parallel to park road. It continues until the turn-around point where the trail meets the park road. This section is nice and wide (approximately 12') with a wooded feel that just beckons a leg stretch.

PENOKEE SCENIC OVERLOOK

Chequamegon-Nicolet National Forest. Off U.S. 2, 64 miles from Superior, 36 miles from Hurley.

- **Sweeping vista of Penokee Mountain range.**
- **Read about the untapped resources of this range.**

DIRECTIONS & PARKING:

From U.S. 2 in Ashland, turn south on WI 13 for 24.2 miles. Turn right (west) on County GG and travel 3 miles to Penokee Overlook right after Chequamegon National Forest sign. You will find a gravel parking lot.

AMENITIES & FEES:
Picnic table with extension, grills, vault toilet (wheelchair accessible). At time of writing, access to toilet was under construction. U.S. Forest vehicle stickers are required to park in this lot or day use fee of $3 (self-pay). Maps are available.

TOTAL TRAIL LENGTH & SURFACE:
0.2 mile; essentially boardwalk.

ALERT:
Please stay on boardwalk.

NARRATIVE:
Trailhead begins at west end of parking lot near sign indicating Scenic Overlook. Ascend 48 steps (wood, double handrail) to platform boardwalk, which features three different overlooks. En route to these overlooks you will encounter an additional 35 steps (wood, double handrail) interspersed along the walk. Spend a little time reading about the Penokee Mountains on the interpretive signs.

 Foot Note:

The Penokees range from southwest of Mellen northeast into Michigan's Upper Peninsula where they are called the Gogebic Range. "Ashland Daily Press" 5/2/00.

LOON LAKE BEACH AREA
Copper Falls State Park • Off U.S. 2, 64 miles from Superior, 36 miles from Hurley

- **Beautiful Loon Lake—a great spot for bird watching.**
- **This trail meets Universal Design Standards.**

DIRECTIONS & PARKING:
From U.S. 2 in Ashland, turn south on WI 13 for 23.8 miles. Turn left (east) on County Road 169 and travel 1.7 miles to Copper Falls State Park. Turn left and follow signs for Red Granite Falls Trail, which is located just a short distance beyond park office. Ample parking available with designated wheelchair accessible parking.

AMENITIES & FEES:
Flush toilets (wheelchair accessible), water, small picnic area, beach house and swimming area. Annual or day use state park permit is required and available at park office.

TOTAL LENGTH/SURFACE:
0.1 mile; paved and constructed to meet Universal Design Standards (see pg. 210 for additional information).

ALERT:
No lifeguard on duty at swimming beach.

NARRATIVE:
Trailhead begins from parking lot on 10'-wide paved path. Continue on path

past beach house toward Loon Lake. Three benches, all on cement pads with grass surface to each, provide lovely views of the lake. There is a small sand beach with buoys marking the swimming area; there is no lifeguard on duty.

SUPERIOR FALLS

Off U.S. 2, 90 miles from Superior, 10 miles from Hurley

- **Superior Falls—on the border of Wisconsin and Michigan.**

DIRECTIONS & PARKING:
From U.S. 2, turn north on WI 122. This road is part of the Lake Superior Circle Tour. Follow for 4.6 miles, crossing the Montreal River into Michigan. Watch for small brown sign for Superior Falls #129. Turn left on gravel road to parking area. Do not park at Xcel Energy Hydro station.

AMENITIES & FEES:
No facilities available. No fees for trail use.

TOTAL LENGTH/SURFACE:
0.1 mile; grass, gravel.

ALERT:
Danger—do not cross fence line.

NARRATIVE:
Trailhead begins from parking area toward Xcel Energy Hydro station. Follow sign for waterfall along fence line. View the Montreal River as it plummets 150' into the river gorge.

UPSON FALLS

Upson • Off U.S. 2, 90 miles from Superior, 10 miles from Hurley

- **Beautiful pristine beauty worth the scramble to see.**
- **Definitely worth taking your camera.**

DIRECTIONS & PARKING:
From U.S. 2, travel 10 miles south on WI 122 to Upson. When road makes an abrupt left turn, make an equally abrupt right turn. This will be Upson Park Road. Drive 0.2 mile to Upson Park, Fire #9475, on left side of road. Paved turnaround in Upson Park.

AMENITIES & FEES:
Vault toilets, water, shelter, campground. No fees for trail use.

TOTAL LENGTH/SURFACE:
0.1 mile; pavement, gravel, hardpacked dirt.

ALERT:
Uneven trail surface. May require scrambling up and down rocky surfaces.

NARRATIVE:
Trailhead begins on paved path off traffic circle then turns right on gravel path. Almost immediately the cascades come into view. For best views, you may need to clamber over some rocks in the path. Use caution.

SHORELINE CLIFFS AND INLAND WOODS*

Jardine Creek Wayside, Port Wing • On WI 13, 39 miles from Superior, 60 miles from Ashland
*Gentle Hikes name

- **A lovely stroll through a short bit of woods yields an extraordinary return with incredible Lake Superior views!**

DIRECTIONS & PARKING:
On WI 13, watch for wayside marker at Fire #5560 on north side of highway. Paved area with designated wheelchair accessible parking available.

AMENITIES & FEES:
Vault toilets (wheelchair accessible), water, picnic tables, grills, benches, map and informational kiosk. No fees for trail use.

TOTAL LENGTH/SURFACE:
800'; paved, grass.

ALERT:
Steep cliffs—stay on trail. Uneven pavement; some tree roots in wooded section. Overgrowth possible in summer.

NARRATIVE:
Trailhead begins at east side of parking area directly in front of water pump. Follow asphalt to the right. Just prior to vault toilets is a trail to the left through the woods. This is a splendid wooded hike that very shortly reveals breathtaking views of Lake Superior. At intersection, turn left onto paved path to return to parking area (trail continues for only a short way to right, but due to significant tree root and erosion, we do not recommend taking it). Expect spectacular views of Lake Superior from this cliff-top vantage point on your return!

PORT WING BOREAL FOREST

Port Wing • On WI 13, 42 miles from Superior, 56 miles from Ashland

- **Off the beaten path, but worth the drive as this location showcases Lake Superior's beautiful rocky and sandy shores.**
- **Lovely views of Port Wing Marina in the distance.**

DIRECTIONS & PARKING:
From WI 13 turn north on Washington Ave at Old School Memorial Park. Drive 0.6 mile to Quarry Road; turn left. Continue 1 mile along this gravel road until

it intersects with Quarry Point Road. Turn right and drive 0.1 mile to small gravel parking area.

AMENITIES & FEES:
None.

TOTAL LENGTH/SURFACE:
90'; hardpacked dirt, sand.

NARRATIVE:
Trailhead begins at sign for Port Wing Boreal Forest, State Natural Area. Just a few yards beyond the boulders bring you to a beautiful sandy shore. This is a favorite of the Port Wing locals who come here during warmer months to enjoy their lunch on the flat rock that juts into the bay. This is a very picturesque area. Bring the camera and if it's summer, hit the beach for some welcome R & R.

IRON BRIDGE ALMOST HIKE*

Bayfield • Off WI 13, 78 miles from Superior, 20 miles from Ashland • *Gentle Hikes name

- **Walk on the historic 230' Iron Bridge built in 1912.**
- **Spectacular view of Lake Superior, Bass and Madeline Islands awaits from the top of the bridge!**
- **View the brook beneath the bridge as it meanders through the luscious fern glades and woods below.**

DIRECTIONS & PARKING:
From WI 13, turn west on County Road I (Washington Avenue). Between 2nd and Broad Streets is a parking area on the north side of the street.

AMENITIES & FEES:
No facilities available. No fees for trail use.

TOTAL LENGTH/SURFACE:
0.3 mile; paved, wood and hardpacked dirt.

ALERT:
Bridge surface uneven in spots.

NARRATIVE:
Trailhead begins at northeast end of parking area. Walk along Washington Avenue (County Road I) toward the lake. You will turn left onto the sidewalk at N. Second Street. Continue up the street and make a left on Rice Avenue, which leads directly to the bridge.

Take a step back in time and enjoy the ambiance of 1920s lightposts and benches that have been restored in memory of loved ones. Enjoy the spectacular view of Lake Superior as well as Bass and Madeline Islands from this historic bridge. Because of deterioration, the bridge was closed to vehicle traffic in1967 and pedestrian traffic in 1983, but was later restored to pedestrian use only, as it remains today. Retrace path to trailhead.

HAUSER'S SUPERIOR VIEW

Bayfield • Off WI 13, 78 miles from Superior, 20 miles from Ashland

- **Sweeping vista of Lake Superior, Long Island, Madeline Island, Big Bay, Porcupine Mountains (Michigan).**
- **Climb to the top of a historic Sears and Roebuck Mail-Order Barn.**

DIRECTIONS & PARKING:
From WI 13 in Bayfield, turn west on County Road I (Washington Avenue). Travel 1.4 miles to County Road J; turn right and drive 0.6 mile to Hauser Orchards on the left. Parking available in unpaved lot in front of red barn.

AMENITIES & FEES:
Gift shop, wine tasting, samples of jams, jellies and salsa, etc., apple tasting (seasonal), field grown perennials, herbs and vegetables (over 250 varieties—seasonal). No fees for trail use.

TOTAL LENGTH/SURFACE:
Up two sets of steps—all wood.

ALERT:
Top of barn can get very hot in summer. Bring water along.

NARRATIVE:
Trailhead begins from parking area near big red barn. Ascend 15 steps (wood, double handrail) to the first observation platform where views of Madeline Island and the Porcupine Mountains of Michigan come into view. But the best is yet to come. Sign the guest registry. Then it's heads-up for the "CAP"ital display and you "CAN"not miss the old beer containers that proudly ring out "99 bottles of beer on the wall, 99 bottles of beer...." Spend a little time in this old Sears and Roebuck Barn, which was built in 1928. Then take the second set of 20 steps (wood, double handrail) to the second observation deck, which puts you 660' above Lake Superior for sweeping views of the lake, Long Island (sandbar to the far left), Madeline Island and Big Bay (both straight ahead) and Porcupine Mountains (Michigan) in the far distance.

SUPERIOR OVERLOOK AT BIG BAY STATE PARK*

Big Bay State Park, Madeline Island • Off WI 13, 78 miles from Superior, 20 miles from Ashland
*Gentle Hikes name

- **Exceptional views of the rugged shoreline of Lake Superior.**

DIRECTIONS & PARKING:
From Ferry Dock on Main Street turn right. Drive two blocks to Middle Road (note brown sign for Big Bay State Park); turn left. Travel 4 miles to stop sign

(road name then changes to Hagen Road). Continue straight for 2 miles and turn left to park office. Head east toward Outdoor Group Camp. Parking is available at Overlook Area. Designated wheelchair accessible parking available.

AMENITIES & FEES:
Picnic tables and bicycle rack. Flush toilets (wheelchair accessible) and water available at park office nearby. Annual or day use state park permit is required and is available at the park office.

TOTAL LENGTH/SURFACE:
315' of fence line trail; grass.

ALERT:
For your safety, stay behind fence as there is erosion at cliff edge.

NARRATIVE:
Trailhead begins at east end of parking area along picturesque wood fence. Simply follow fence line until it ends. Take your time as the views are breathtaking. On a clear day, look in the distance for the Porcupine Mountains of Michigan's Upper Peninsula. The brown and green trimmed cabin directly behind parking area is of historical significance. John Hagen (Hagen Road) built it and the park has restored it to be historically accurate.

BIG BAY POINT*

Big Bay State Park, Madeline Island • Off WI 13, 78 miles from Superior, 20 miles from Ashland
*Gentle Hikes name

- **Glorious overlook of the rugged cliff face that characterizes this portion of Lake Superior.**
- **Walk through an old growth forest with hemlocks 200–300 years old!**

DIRECTIONS & PARKING:
From Ferry Dock on Main Street turn right. Drive two blocks to Middle Road (note brown sign for Big Bay State Park); turn left. Travel 4 miles to stop sign (road name then changes to Hagen Road). Continue straight for 2 miles and turn left to park office. At first park stop sign turn right toward Campground, Picnic Area and Beach. At next stop sign turn right toward Big Bay Point. Continue on road past Picnic Area and Beach to paved parking loop. Wheelchair accessible parking, moped parking and bike racks available.

AMENITIES & FEES:
Vault toilets (wheelchair accessible) 150' into trail, water, Big Bay Point Picnic Area (see pg. 194). Annual or day use state park permit is required and is available at the park office.

TOTAL LENGTH/SURFACE:
0.3 mile; hardpacked dirt.

ALERT:
Steep cliffs—stay on trail.

NARRATIVE:

Trailhead begins at east end of parking area near self pay box. Enter through an old growth forest and into a gorgeous stand of hemlock (some are 200–300 years old!). You will find several picnic tables scattered about. In 150' restrooms will be to the left. At time of writing (August 2003) there was a very intriguing sight just prior to a trail intersection near a picnic table toward the right. Branches had been woven together to form a hut-like structure under a tree. If still there, it's worth a look.

Continue straight another 100' to the overlook marked by a wooden fence. This is Big Bay Point and offers a grand view of Lake Superior's rugged shoreline and cliffs. There is also a unique stone bench on the point that is very picturesque.

If a busload of people should wander out to the Point while you are there, they are most likely part of the Island Bus Tour group. The authors have taken the tour and recommend it to anyone wanting a good overview and historical information regarding Madeline Island. Not only does the tour showcase this Almost Hike, it offers the option of hiking the Bay View Trail (pg. 118), which is also featured in this book. For more information see Foot Note below.

 Foot Note:

Should you desire to leave your car on the mainland and take the ferry to Madeline Island, there is a 2-hour Bus Tour (seasonal) given by local guides. Even if you brought the car, it's still a fun way to get an overview of the island. Call (715) 747-2051 for more information.

BARRIER BEACH*

Big Bay State Park, Madeline Island • Off WI 13, 78 miles from Superior, 20 miles from Ashland
*Gentle Hikes name

- **Gorgeous views of Big Bay from Barrier Beach.**
- **Popular swimming spot in summer.**

DIRECTIONS & PARKING:

From Ferry Dock on Main Street turn right. Drive two blocks to Middle Road (note brown sign for Big Bay State Park); turn left. Travel 4 miles to stop sign (road name then changes to Hagen Road). Continue straight for 2 miles and turn left to park office. At first park stop sign turn right toward Campground, Picnic Area and Beach. At next stop sign turn right toward Picnic Area and Beach, then left to Barrier Beach and paved parking lot. Wheelchair accessible parking, moped parking and bike racks available.

AMENITIES & FEES:

Vault toilets (wheelchair accessible), water, changing stalls, picnic area (see Barrier Beach Picnic Area pg. 193). Annual or day use state park permit is required and is available at the park office.

TOTAL LENGTH/SURFACE:
0.2 mile; grass, steps and soft sand.

ALERT:
Uneven surface under last step. No bicycles or pets due to beach area. No lifeguard on duty.

NARRATIVE:
Trailhead begins on paved path at north end of parking area toward restrooms. Behind restrooms, head toward water pump, which is in the middle of the field. There is no trail here. The blue shed and fire ring area to the left are used for the park's interpretive programs (see kiosk near shed for schedule). If identifying wildflowers, birds and ferns interest you, the park has brochures available (as well as park maps) free of charge in a wooden box near this location. Continue walking toward the lake and find stairs tucked between a bench and maple tree. Descend 45 steps (wood, double handrail) to beach area. Several logs sculpted by Superior's touch serve as benches for beachside relaxation.

BIG BAY TOWN PARK LAGOON*

Madeline Island • Off WI 13, 78 miles from Superior, 20 miles from Ashland • *Gentle Hikes name

---

- **Gorgeous overlook of Big Bay Lagoon.**

DIRECTIONS & PARKING:
From Ferry Dock on Main Street turn left. Follow Main Street around right curve. It will become Big Bay Road and County Road H. At intersection with North Shore Road stay to right on County Road H. Continue past Black's Shanty Road for 2 miles. Follow green sign for Big Bay Town Park. Turn right into Town Park and left to beach parking in sand and gravel lot. Designated wheelchair accessible parking available.

AMENITIES & FEES:
Vault toilets (wheelchair accessible), water, picnic area (see Big Bay Town Park Picnic Area pg. 194).

TOTAL LENGTH/SURFACE:
320'; sand and gravel, grass.

ALERT:
Steep dropoff at overlook. There are numerous campsites near parking lot; please be respectful of campers.

NARRATIVE:
Trailhead begins at east end of parking lot on 10'-wide sand and gravel path past picnic area. Find a bench to the right that provides a near perfect overlook of Big Bay Lagoon. This is a very picturesque area in and of itself and if there are canoes and kayaks on the water, it's just a scenic bonus. This view ends our Almost Hike. There is so much more to this area if you are up for a trek down the stairs and onto the trail (see Big Bay Town Park Trail, pg. 128).

NOT-TO-BE-MISSED PANORAMIC BAY STROLL*

Washburn • Off WI 13, 91 miles from Superior, 7 miles from Ashland • *Gentle Hikes name

- **One of the few places on the shore to showcase a nearly 360° sweep of Chequamegon Bay and Lake Superior in the distance.**

DIRECTIONS & PARKING:

From WI 13, turn south on 8th Avenue W toward Lake Superior. Drive 0.3 mile through residential neighborhood to gravel parking area.

AMENITIES & FEES:

Flush toilets (wheelchair accessible) in campground, water, picnic area (see Thompson's West End Picnic Area pg. 195). No fees for trail use.

TOTAL LENGTH/SURFACE:

0.1 mile; gravel, dirt.

ALERT:

None at time of writing.

NARRATIVE:

Trailhead begins from unpaved parking lot between picnic area and fishing dock. This little path delivers big on a view with a nearly panoramic eyeful of the Chequamegon Bay. Look for the Apostle Islands on a clear day. This vantage point serves up some wonderful photo ops with its tiny islands and intriguing rock formations.

LONG LAKE PICNIC STROLL*

Chequamegon-Nicolet National Forest • Off WI 13, 93 miles from Superior, 5 miles from Ashland
*Gentle Hikes name

- **Beautiful Long Lake!**

DIRECTIONS & PARKING:

From WI 13 south of Washburn turn west on Wanabo Road (various spellings, e.g., Wannebo, Wanabo, Wanebo). Travel 6 miles to sign for Chequamegon National Forest Picnic Grounds, Long Lake; turn right. Drive 0.1 mile to sign for Long Lake picnic grounds, boat landing; turn left and continue to paved parking lot. Ample parking available with designated wheelchair accessible parking.

AMENITIES & FEES:

Vault toilets (wheelchair accessible), water, picnic area (see Long Lake Picnic Area pg. 196), beach. U.S. Forest vehicle stickers are required to park in this lot or day use fee of $3 (self-pay).

TOTAL LENGTH/SURFACE:

0.2 mile; paved.

ALERT:

No lifeguard on duty at swimming beach.

NARRATIVE:

Trailhead begins from parking lot on paved path that circles around wooded picnic area and offers lovely views of Long Lake. Bring a picnic lunch to enjoy after your stroll.

Iron Bridge Almost Hike (pg. 165). Photo by Melanie Morgan

WAYSIDES & SCENIC LOCALES

We have included the most scenic waysides and overlooks that Lake Superior's South Shore and northern Wisconsin have to offer. Includes stuff you don't even need to leave the car to see!

We tell you which are paved and which have designated wheelchair accessible and RV parking, plus highlights, amenities and a brief narrative of what to expect while there.

Keep in mind that many waysides are closed during snow season. Some only operate seasonally (mid-May to mid-October). This being northern Wisconsin, these are close approximations based on ground freezing and thawing.

Don't forget the camera!

Jardine Creek Wayside (pg. 179). Photo by Melanie Morgan

OLD STOCKADE SITE WAYSIDE*

Superior • On U.S. 2, 1 mile from Superior-Douglas County Visitor Center • *Gentle Hikes name

- **Historical marker regarding summer of 1862 and history of this site.**
- **Lovely view of Barker's Island Harbor.**

DIRECTIONS & PARKING:

From U.S. 2 at the Superior-Douglas County Visitor Center drive southeast 1 mile to traffic lights at 18th Avenue E. Turn toward the bay and brown Historical Marker into paved parking area. Designated wheelchair accessible parking available.

AMENITIES:

Picnic tables, benches, gazebo.

NARRATIVE:

Interesting historical marker, time capsule and various information engraved on stones throughout make this a wonderful stop for history buffs. It's also a great spot for a leg stretcher as this not only offers access to the Osaugie Trail (see Old Stockade Site to Loonsfoot Landing pg. 40), but provides a short loop trail (a trail within a trail, so to speak) of approximately 800' roundtrip. To take the loop, head for the historical marker regarding this site and take the lower paved trail closer to the water. Turn right (Osaugie continues to the left also; see Superior Bay to Trail Beginning pg. 32) and continue 400' until you reach the first intersection, which loops back onto the upper portion of the Osaugie Trail and parking area.

NORTHWEST PORTAL OF WISCONSIN WAYSIDE

Superior • On U.S. 2, 5 miles from Superior-Douglas County Visitor Center, 95 miles from Hurley

- **Well stocked information center with weather reports.**
- **Nice spread of picnic tables.**

DIRECTIONS & PARKING:
On west side of U.S. 2 between Moccasin Mike Road and WI 13 find Rest Area and Wisconsin Tourist Information Center. Paved parking area with designated wheelchair accessible and RV parking available.

AMENITIES:
Flush toilets (wheelchair accessible), water, picnic tables, grills, phones, TV/weather, vending machines, recycling bins.

NARRATIVE:
Well stocked and staffed Visitor Center with informational kiosk and many brochures. Several picnic tables spread out in a beautiful grassy, semi-wooded area make this a nice stopping place.

BRULE RIVER WAYSIDE*

Brule • On U.S. 2, 28 miles from Superior, 72 miles from Hurley • *Gentle Hikes name

- **Historical marker about the Brule River.**
- **Picturesque river views (see Brule River View Almost Hike pg. 158).**

DIRECTIONS & PARKING:
On U.S. 2 in Brule, locate lovely wayside on south side of highway. Paved parking available with designated wheelchair accessible and RV spaces.

AMENITIES:
Vault toilets (wheelchair accessible), water, picnic tables, grills, map kiosk.

NARRATIVE:
Worth the quick stop to read a little about the Brule River's history, formation and the activity that surrounded it in the past.

IRON RIVER WAYSIDE*

Iron River • On U.S. 2, 38 miles from Superior, 62 miles from Hurley • *Gentle Hikes name

- **Lovely lake view just yards off the highway.**

DIRECTIONS & PARKING:
Located on U.S. 2 just west of Iron River, watch for blue sign for rest area/wayside. Paved parking area with designated wheelchair accessible and RV parking.

AMENITIES:

Vault toilets (wheelchair accessible), water, picnic tables, grills, benches, map kiosk.

NARRATIVE:

Easy access from highway makes for a great place to rest with nice scenery. Break out the snacks or lunch and dine under a splendid canopy of oak, pine and maple as you soak up lake views.

OVERLOOK PARK WAYSIDE

Ashland • On U.S. 2, 64 miles from Superior, 36 miles from Hurley

* **Sweeping vista of Lake Superior's Chequamagen Bay.**
* **Intriguing distance legend at west end.**

DIRECTIONS & PARKING:

On U.S. 2, this location may be a little difficult to find. It is tucked next to a gas station between 10th and 11th Avenues W on the lakeside. Watch for turn in to small paved parking area with designated wheelchair accessible parking.

AMENITIES:

Picnic tables and benches.

NARRATIVE:

See the site where Whittlesey and Kilborn felled the first tree cut in Ashland on July 5, 1854. It was used as part of the foundation for the first house built in Ashland (by Whittlesey). The distance legend points you in the direction of a variety of locations, such as the Apostle Islands, etc., and on a clear day some may be visible.

MEMORIAL PARK WAYSIDE*

Ashland • On U.S. 2, 64 miles from Superior, 36 miles from Hurley • *Gentle Hikes name

* **Memorial Park commemorates local men and women who served in the Armed Forces. Read about the commercial logging industry of eras past.**
* **Lovely vista of Ashland marina (telescope available), wheelchair accessible.**

DIRECTIONS & PARKING:

Located on U.S. 2, this is an easy location to find just west of the park and the Chequamegon Hotel. Watch for turn-in to small paved parking area (accessible from east end only). Designated wheelchair accessible parking available.

AMENITIES:

Picnic tables, benches, bandshell.

NARRATIVE:

This wayside delivers big on lovely views of Lake Superior's Chequamagen Bay. Try out the telescope that allows you to focus fairly close on waterfowl. Spend some time at Memorial Park reading the historical markers. Paved walk to bandshell.

HISTORICAL MARKER OF THE BAD RIVER

Odanah • On U.S. 2, 74 miles from Superior, 26 miles from Hurley

- **Discover how the Bad River acquired its name as well as other notable historical events.**

DIRECTIONS & PARKING:
On U.S. 2, look for sign indicating Historical Marker. Pull into paved area.

AMENITIES:
None.

NARRATIVE:
A short pull-through off U.S. 2 gives quick access to a brief historical account of the establishment of three Native American reservations: Odanah, Lac Court Oreilles and Lac du Flambeau.

APOSTLE ISLANDS SCENIC OVERLOOK

Saxon • On U.S. 2, 90 miles from Superior, 10 miles from Hurley

- **Sweeping vista of Apostle Islands and Chequamegon Bay.**

DIRECTIONS & PARKING:
On U.S. 2, watch for blue sign indicating Scenic Overlook. Pull into paved parking area (no trucks).

AMENITIES:
None.

NARRATIVE:
Worth the stop on a clear day! An interpretive map display gives geographical locations as well as information about the 22 Apostle Islands, which form an archipelago about 30 miles long and 18 miles wide.

GOGEBIC IRON RANGE WAYSIDE

Saxon • On U.S. 2, 91 miles from Superior, 9 miles from Hurley

- **Historical information about the Gogebic Iron Range and the iron mining industry in the late 1800s.**
- **Sweeping vistas of the Range that runs for 80 miles.**

DIRECTIONS & PARKING:
On U.S. 2, look for sign indicating Historical Marker. Paved parking available with designated RV parking.

AMENITIES:
One small open-sided picnic shelter with a table.

NARRATIVE:

Highly scenic and great place for a leg stretch!

WISCONSIN TRAVEL INFORMATION CENTER

Hurley • Off U.S. 2, 100 miles from Superior

- **Visitor center packed with brochures and information, plus the added bonus of mining artifacts and history.**

DIRECTIONS & PARKING:

From U.S. 2 just outside of Hurley, follow U.S. 51 south to Information Center. Turn into paved parking area. Designated wheelchair and RV parking available.

AMENITIES:

Flush toilets (wheelchair accessible), water, picnic tables, open-sided shelter.

NARRATIVE:

Plethora of information and helpful staff make this a great place to plan your Wisconsin stay. Well maintained grounds as well. Furthermore, there's an opportunity to step back in time and see things through the eyes of a miner with photos, history and artifacts as interpretive guides. Happy traveling!

JARDINE CREEK WAYSIDE*

Port Wing • On WI 13, 39 miles from Superior, 60 miles from Ashland • *Gentle Hikes name

- **Incredible views of Lake Superior.**

DIRECTIONS & PARKING:
On WI 13, watch for wayside marker at Fire #5560 on north side of highway. Paved area with designated wheelchair accessible parking available.

AMENITIES:
Vault toilets (wheelchair accessible), water, picnic tables, grills, benches, map and informational kiosk.

NARRATIVE:
Some of the best views of Lake Superior await the traveler at this wayside. This highly scenic area is an excellent place to have lunch or just stretch your legs. Be sure to take the Shoreline Cliffs and Inland Woods Almost Hike (pg. 164).

OLD SCHOOL MEMORIAL PARK*

Port Wing • On WI 13, 42 miles from Superior, 56 miles from Ashland • *Gentle Hikes name

- **A delightful journey around the block yields memories of yesteryear as originals and replicas from Wisconsin and Port Wing's past are featured here.**

DIRECTIONS & PARKING:
On WI 13 in Port Wing, look for sign indicating Historical Marker. Pull in along side street at park.

AMENITIES:
Picnic table, grills, benches, playground.

NARRATIVE:
To step back into Wisconsin's history, you won't have to go very far. The trek around the block features a replica of the very first school rig in the state, mail sleds, Heritage Hall, Port Wing jail from 1896 and the original Old School Bell. Have fun and bring the family!

SISKIWIT BAY PARK & WAYSIDE

Cornucopia • On WI 13, 58 miles from Superior, 40 miles from Ashland

- **Incredible views of Lake Superior and warm sandy beaches.**
- **Tour the Historical Museum and visit the various shops near marina.**
- **Fill up your cup from the artesian well under gazebo.**

DIRECTIONS & PARKING:
Located on WI 13 in Cornucopia, watch for wayside on north side of highway, Fire #22745. Turn into gravel parking area.

AMENITIES:

Flush toilet (wheelchair accessible), artesian well, picnic tables, grills, shelters, playground, volleyball court, marina, gift shops.

NARRATIVE:

Welcome to the warm, sandy beaches of the south shore of Lake Superior. This is a marvelous place to view the lake anytime, but spectacular for a sunset over Roman Point! Spend some time here reading the history of Siskiwit Bay (marker located north of gazebo) and exploring the historical museum. Gift shops and points of interest abound in this quaint little area so make sure you head over to the marina.

Siskiwit Bay Wayside (pg. 179). Photo by Ladona Tornabene

PICNIC AREAS

Whether you grill it or pack it, we have selected some of the most scenic picnic areas along Lake Superior's South Shore and in northern Wisconsin. From woods to rivers and the big lake, you'll find all kinds of picnic spots listed here. Bon appetit!

We had a little fun writing the picnic areas in a "Menu" format featuring 'Appetizers,' 'Main Course,' and 'Dessert.'

APPETIZER:

Typically we list what is nearby and en route to the picnic area (what precedes it—as an appetizer precedes a meal), be it an Almost Hike, trail or wayside.

MAIN COURSE:

Here's where we describe what the actual picnic area is like.

DESSERT:

Usually we list what is nearby the picnic area—be it an Almost Hike, trail or area to explore. It's what we recommend as a great finish to a good meal, but actually burns calories instead!

In addition, we include amenities (located at the picnic area sites), applicable fees, parking surface and designated wheelchair accessible spaces.

Please note: All tables are park and carry.

Bois Brule Picnic Area (pg. 189). Photo by Ladona Tornabene

BARKER'S ISLAND PICNIC AREA

Superior • Off U.S. 2, 0.1 mile from Superior-Douglas County Visitor Center

- **Appetizer: Take the Welcome-A-Board-Walk Almost Hike (pg. 152) for an overview of island attractions.**

- **Main Course: Kudos for the design layout here! Each table is located in a semi-wooded environment and has its own entry path with ample distance from the other picnic sites. It's like picnicking on your own private pad.**

- **Dessert: This is a wonderfully scenic area as Superior Bay beckons. Heed the call with the Barker's Island Trail (pg. 30), which serves generous helpings of bay views.**

PICNIC AREA DIRECTIONS & PARKING:

From U.S. 2 at the Superior-Douglas County Visitor Center turn east onto service road beside Visitor Center and Bong WWII Heritage Center. Follow signs indicating Barker's Island. You will see a big paved parking area near the *SS Meteor* but continue past green billboard on entrance road to the right and find picnic areas with paved parking spaces near sites (first spot has wheelchair designated space; RV parking nearby). There are several tables with separate walk-in entry points spanning a distance of 0.1 mile.

AMENITIES & FEES:

Flush toilets (located in the *SS Meteor* but has same hours as gift shops), portable toilet (wheelchair accessible), water fountain, playground—all located off main parking lot. Each table has a grill. There is a small beach (no lifeguard) near last picnic area. No fees for picnic use.

BARKER'S ISLAND PLAY AREA PICNIC AREA

Superior • Off U.S. 2, 0.1 mile from Superior-Douglas County Visitor Center

- **Appetizer: Have a whale of a time on the Welcome-A-Board-Walk Almost Hike (pg. 152) and while you're there, look at your dessert choices.**

- **Main Course: Even if you didn't pack a lunch, there are eateries in the area. Dine at tables in the playground or pick one closer to Superior Bay for spectacular views.**

- **Dessert: And the dessert tray is as follows: Your choice of relaxing on the Vista Fleet Cruise, which docks right across from the playground; touring the last whaleback ship in the world, the *SS Meteor*; challenging the family to a game of mini golf or browsing the gift shops. Ahoy!**

PICNIC AREA DIRECTIONS & PARKING:

From U.S. 2 at the Superior-Douglas County Visitor Center turn east onto service road beside Visitor Center and Bong WWII Heritage Center. Follow signs indicating Barker's Island. Continue to paved parking area near *SS Meteor*. Designated RV and wheelchair accessible spaces.

AMENITIES & FEES:
Flush toilets (located in the *SS Meteor* but has same hours as gift shops), portable toilet (wheelchair accessible), water fountain, playground. No fees for picnic area use.

 Foot Note:

Information on touring the *SS Meteor* can be found on pg. 153. To take one of a variety of cruises on the Vista Fleet call (218) 722-6218 or www.vistafleet.com

BILLINGS PARK PICNIC AREA

Superior • Off U.S. 2, 4 miles from Superior-Douglas County Visitor Center

- **Appetizer: Take Rhonda and Joe's Wedding Stroll Almost Hike (pg. 152) to scope out the best spot for picnicking.**
- **Main Course: Many tables to choose among, from the pavilion to the wooded paths.**
- **Dessert: Soak up gorgeous views of the St. Louis Bay on the Riverfront Trail (pg. 28).**

PICNIC AREA DIRECTIONS & PARKING:
From the Superior-Douglas County Visitor Center head east on U.S. 2 for 1.7 miles. At Tower Ave (WI 35) turn left (south) and travel 0.5 mile to 21st Street. Turn right (west) and travel 1.6 miles to sign for Billings Park; drive around traffic circle to Billings Drive. Turn right and continue to next Billings Park sign and arrow pointing to the right. Turn here and drive to small paved lot at end of in-drive. Parking is also allowed on one side of drive—please note signs.

AMENITIES & FEES:
Flush toilets (wheelchair accessible), water spigot, pavilion, open-sided shelter, water fountain, grills, volleyball court, small gardens, horseshoe pits, playground and unique playground for those with disabilities.

BEAR CREEK PARK

Superior • On U.S. 2, 5 miles from Superior-Douglas County Visitor Center, 95 miles from Hurley

- **Appetizer: Warm up with a friendly game of basketball or softball.**
- **Main Course: Picnic near a fun play place with a nice covered shelter.**
- **Dessert: Take the scenic drive out to Wisconsin Point for our Wisconsin Point Lighthouse Almost Hike (pg. 153) or Superior Entry Almost Hike (pg. 154).**

PICNIC AREA DIRECTIONS & PARKING:

On U.S. 2 at the point where the highway splits and becomes a divided four lane, turn north on Mocassin Mike Road, then left into gravel parking area. Paved path extends 90' to shelter.

AMENITIES & FEES:

Portable toilet (seasonal), playground, basketball court, softball field, open-sided shelter, grills. No fees for picnic area use.

 Foot Note:

Superior's Sister City is Ami-Machi, Japan.

BIG MANITOU FALLS PICNIC AREA

Pattison State Park • Off U.S. 2, 13 miles south of Superior

- **Appetizer: Whet your appetite for scenic beauty by taking the Big Manitou Falls Almost Hike (pg. 155) to the highest waterfall in Wisconsin.**

- **Main Course: Lovely wooded picnic area is prime spot for an auditory buffet as you dine amid maple and oak within yards of the thunderous falls.**

- **Dessert: To top off your meal with more waterfall action, drive down to Little Falls Hiking Trail (pg. 54).**

PICNIC AREA DIRECTIONS & PARKING:

From the Superior-Douglas County Visitor Center head west on U.S. 2 for 1.7 miles. Turn left (south) on WI 35 (Tower Ave) and travel 13 miles. Drive 0.1 mile past sign for Pattison State Park. Turn right onto County Road B and almost immediately turn left into paved parking lot. Designed wheelchair accessible parking available. Take paved trail leading out of parking area—use caution when crossing County Road B; pick up trail by sign indicating Pedestrian Crossing. Paved path is uneven due to tree root protrusions.

AMENITIES & FEES:

Vault toilets, grills. Annual or day use state park permit is required and is available at the park office.

PATTISON STATE PARK MAIN PICNIC AREA

Pattison State Park • Off U.S. 2, 13 miles south of Superior

- **Appetizer: Have some fun at the outdoor fitness station or try your hand at a game of horseshoes.**

- **Main Course:** Truly spectacular views of Interfalls Lake abound with a plethora of tables from which to choose. Dining also available inside fully enclosed shelter.

- **Dessert:** Definitely save room for this one! Stroll through the Gitche Gumee Nature Center, which exhibits fabulous interpretive displays on park and natural history as well as birds, fish and other animals. A must-see.

PICNIC AREA DIRECTIONS & PARKING:

From the Superior-Douglas County Visitor Center head west on U.S. 2 for 1.7 miles. Turn left (south) on WI 35 (Tower Ave) and travel 13 miles. Watch for sign for Pattison State Park. Turn left to park office. Ample parking with designated RV and wheelchair accessible parking available.

AMENITIES & FEES:

Park office has small gift shop, flush toilet (wheelchair accessible), water vending machines, nature center with two fireplaces, fitness station, playground, volleyball, horseshoe pit, basketball hoop, beach on the lake, pay phone. Annual or day use state park permit is required and available at park office.

LITTLE MANITOU FALLS PICNIC AREA

Pattison State Park • Off U.S. 2, 14 miles south of Superior

- **Appetizer:** Whet your appetite with glorious views of Little Manitou Falls.

- **Main Course:** Dine near the former site of Camp Pattison Mess Hall. Although no longer at this site, it was the most popular place at camp.

- **Dessert:** Be adventurous. Take the entire Little Falls Hiking Trail that hugs the Black River.

PICNIC AREA DIRECTIONS & PARKING:

From the Superior-Douglas County Visitor Center head west on U.S. 2 for 1.7 miles. Turn left (south) on WI 35 (Tower Ave) and travel 13 miles. Watch for sign for Pattison State Park. Continue on WI 35 for 1 additional mile south of main entrance to Pattison State Park. Follow sign and turn left to paved parking areas. Lower lot has designated RV and wheelchair accessible parking. Upper lot has wheelchair accessible parking and access to canoe pullout.

AMENITIES & FEES:

Vault toilets, water, grills, swings. Canoe access and portage location. Annual or day use state park permit is required and is available at the park office.

 Foot Note:

During the Depression, 60% of CCC enrollees were underweight; however, by the end of their second month in camp, average weight gain per enrollee was 11 pounds. (Wisconsin Department of Natural Resources)

AMNICON FALLS STATE PARK
SHELTERED PICNIC AREA*

Amnicon Falls State Park • Off U.S. 2, 12 miles from Superior, 87 miles from Hurley • *Gentle Hikes Name

- **Appetizer: Take the Amnicon Wooded and Riverview Stroll Almost Hike (pg. 158).**
- **Main Course: Your choice of tables under open-sided shelter or under the trees.**
- **Dessert: Take the interpretive Amnicon Falls Geology Walk (pg. 56) for unbeatable views of three waterfalls!**

PICNIC AREA DIRECTIONS & PARKING:

On U.S. 2, turn north on County Road U for 0.3 mile; turn left at sign for Amnicon Falls State Park. From office parking area turn left at stop sign, then right and over bridge, following signs for Campground and Nature Trail. Drive 0.1 mile to small paved parking area on right near open-sided shelter. RV parking is available here or at next paved lot, which is 0.1 mile further.

AMENITIES & FEES:

Water, grills, swingset. Annual or day use state park permit is required and available at park office.

AMNICON FALLS STATE PARK
ACCESSIBLE PICNIC AREA*

Amnicon Falls State Park • Off U.S. 2, 12 miles from Superior, 87 miles from Hurley • *Gentle Hikes Name

- **Appetizer: Take the Amnicon Falls Wooded and Riverview Stroll Almost Hike through a lovely wooded area (pg. 158) on a wide, flat path.**
- **Main Course: River view dining with accessible table and paved access.**
- **Dessert: Enjoy the sights and sounds of the beautiful Amnicon River.**

PICNIC AREA DIRECTIONS & PARKING:

On U.S. 2, turn north on County Road U for 0.3 mile; turn left at sign for Amnicon Falls State Park. From office parking area turn left at stop sign, then right and over bridge, following signs for Campground and Nature Trail. Drive 0.2 mile to second small paved parking area on right, beyond open-sided shelter. RV parking is available here or at first paved lot 0.1 mile back.

AMENITIES & FEES:

Vault toilet (wheelchair accessible), water nearby, grill. Annual or day use state park permit is required and available at park office.

BOIS BRULE PICNIC AREA

Brule River State Forest • Off U.S. 2, 28 miles from Superior, 72 miles from Hurley

- **Appetizer: Indulge your appetite for nature on a spectacular interpretive trail (Stony Hill Nature Trail, pg. 66).**
- **Main Course: Dine in a wooded setting with views of the beautiful Brule River and Bois Brule Landing.**
- **Dessert: Relax and listen to the babble of the Brule on a perfectly placed bench at river's edge.**

PICNIC AREA DIRECTIONS & PARKING:

From U.S. 2 in Brule, turn south on Anderson Road—the road immediately east of the Brule River Wayside. At sign for State Forest Campground continue straight; at next intersection turn right and follow to paved circular parking area with designated wheelchair accessible and RV spaces.

AMENITIES & FEES:

Grills, fire ring, benches. Vault toilet (wheelchair accessible) and drinking water are available in the adjacent campground. Designated canoe landing location for campground patrons. A state parks and forest admission sticker is required (self-pay box). These are one and the same if you have a Wisconsin State Park sticker.

 Foot Note:

"The excellent water quality of the Brule River can be attributed to the forest ecosystem, which surrounds the springs that supply the water to the upper river." (WI DNR 2002)

PRENTICE PARK PICNIC AREA

Ashland • Off U.S. 2, 62 miles from Superior, 38 miles from Hurley

- **Appetizer: Take the Cedar Edge Loop for picture-worthy lagoon views and waterfowl variety (pg. 78)**
- **Main Course: Several tables scattered throughout this park range from the covered shelter to wooded settings.**
- **Dessert: Sample the artesian well water as you head out to Artesian Way (pg. 76).**

PICNIC AREA DIRECTIONS & PARKING:

From U.S. 2 in the west end of Ashland, watch for large brown sign indicating City of Ashland Prentice Park. This can be found near Maslowski Beach. Turn south at sign on Turner Road and drive 0.2 mile to next sign. Turn right and continue to paved parking area near picnic pavilion. Designated RV and wheelchair accessible parking.

AMENITIES & FEES:

Flush toilets (wheelchair accessible), water. No fees for picnic area usage.

MASLOWSKI BEACH PICNIC AREA

Maslowski Beach • On U.S. 2, 62 miles from Superior, 38 miles from Hurley

- **Appetizer: Take some time to read about the Radisson-Groseilliers cabin, which is located in the parking area.**

- **Main Course: Dine with glorious unobstructed views of Lake Superior's Chequamegan Bay. Your choice of seating near picturesque beach or under open-sided shelter.**

- **Dessert: To top off your meal, take a stroll down the Ashland Bayfront Trail (pg. 82). This is where the entire trail begins.**

PICNIC AREA DIRECTIONS & PARKING:

Located on U.S. 2, this is an easy location to find. Watch for brown sign indicating City of Ashland, Maslowski Beach; turn in to paved parking area. Ample space available in two lots; east lot has designated wheelchair accessible parking; west lot has paved access to the picnic shelter.

AMENITIES & FEES:

Flush toilets (wheelchair accessible), artesian well, grills, playground, swimming beach (no lifeguard on duty), beach house, pay phone, bike rack. No fees for picnic area usage.

KREHAR PARK PICNIC AREA

Ashland • On U.S. 2, 64 miles from Superior, 36 miles from Hurley

- **Appetizer: Work up an appetite by taking a stroll along the Ashland Bayfront Trail, Krehar Park to Water Plant (pg. 90), which can be accessed from this parking area.**

- **Main Course: Your choice of dining within yards of the beach area, on the grounds or under an open-sided shelter with views of Chequamegan Bay.**

- **Dessert: Let your cup run over! Take a short walk over to the artesian well near the park entrance.**

PICNIC AREA DIRECTIONS & PARKING:

From U.S. 2, turn northwest on Prentice Ave (between 3rd and 5th Avenues E) toward Chequamegon Bay and follow for 0.1 mile to park entrance. Ample paved parking available with designated wheelchair accessible and RV spaces.

AMENITIES & FEES:

Flush toilets (wheelchair accessible), water, grills, playground, swimming beach, fishing pier, boat launch, pay phone, RV designated campground (no tents). No fees for picnic area/trail usage, but $20 fee per day for campground (self-pay).

COPPER FALLS STATE PARK MAIN PICNIC AREA

Copper Falls State Park • Off U.S. 2, 64 miles from Superior, 36 miles from Hurley

- **Appetizer: Work up an appetite with the trek up to Observation Tower (pg. 98) for panoramic views of Apostle Islands, Chequamagen Bay and sand cliffs.**
- **Main Course: Smorgasbord of tables (some constructed of beautiful log) to choose from in an open, wooded setting or partially enclosed shelter. Very nice. Even if you forgot to pack a lunch, you're in luck. There is a concession stand on the premises.**
- **Dessert: Take in the splendor of Copper and Brownstone Falls on the Three Bridges Trail (pg. 94). Afterward, have a treat from the concession stand (scrumptious ice cream!).**

PICNIC AREA DIRECTIONS & PARKING:

From U.S. 2 in Ashland, turn south on WI 13 for 23.8 miles. Turn left (east) on County Road 169 and travel 1.7 miles to Copper Falls State Park. Turn left to park office; follow signs for Copper Falls and Brownstone Falls, which are about 1 mile beyond park office. Ample parking available in paved lot with designated wheelchair accessible parking.

AMENITIES & FEES:

Flush toilets (wheelchair accessible), water, benches, playground, gift shop/concessions (seasonal). Annual or day use state park permit is required.

BAYVIEW PARK PICNIC AREA

Bayview Park • On U.S. 2, 65 miles from Superior, 35 miles from Hurley

- **Appetizer: Catch your lunch! Take a stroll out to the bay via a red brick path to the fishing pier.**
- **Main Course: Wide variety of dining options. Choose from tables literally within feet of Chequamegen Bay, or those perched on viewing platforms, or those tucked under an open-sided shelter. All afford spectacular views of Lake Superior's Chequamegen Bay and on a clear day, the Apostle Islands.**
- **Dessert: Take the Ashland Bayfront Trail (pg. 92), which can be accessed from this parking area.**

PICNIC AREA DIRECTIONS & PARKING:

Located on U.S. 2, this is an easy location to find across from the shopping center. Watch for turn-in to paved parking. Ample space available in two lots. The east lot is bigger. Both have designated wheelchair accessible parking. The west lot has paved access to the picnic shelter and a small viewing deck.

Flush toilets (wheelchair accessible), water, grills, playground, wheelchair accessible parking. Annual or day use state park permit is required and available at park office.

SAXON HARBOR PICNIC AREA

Lake Superior County Park • Off U.S. 2, 90 miles from Superior, 10 miles from Hurley

* **Appetizer: Take the Superior Falls Almost Hike (pg. 163).**

* **Main Course: Dine under an irresistibly quaint shelter overlooking Lake Superior or choose from tables scattered about the park. Screened pavilion can be reserved for large groups.**

* **Dessert: Soak it all up! Picturesque sandy cliffs guard the beaches of Superior.**

PICNIC AREA DIRECTIONS & PARKING:

From U.S. 2, turn north on WI 122. This road is part of the Lake Superior Circle Tour. Follow to County Road A; turn left (west) and continue to Saxon Harbor. There are numerous paved parking areas.

AMENITIES & FEES:

Vault toilets (wheelchair accessible), water, grills, playground, boat launch, benches, pay phone, volleyball court, camping, safe harbor. Fees for park use, camping and boat launch (self-pay boxes).

Mouth of the Brule River Picnic Area (pg. 193). Photo by Lisa Vogelsang

MOUTH OF THE BRULE RIVER PICNIC AREA

Brule River State Forest • Off WI 13, 31 miles from Superior, 67 miles from Ashland

- **Appetizer: Take time to read a marker in the picnic area that tells about historical activity on the Brule.**
- **Main Course: Incredible Lake Superior views!**
- **Dessert: Descend the 27 steps (wood, no handrail—use caution as some may be loose) to the beach area to see where the Brule joins Lake Superior. A beautiful area in and of itself, but also a popular fishing spot—well worth the short walk.**

PICNIC AREA DIRECTIONS & PARKING:

From WI 13, turn west on gravel road at sign for Lake Superior and Mouth of the Brule River. Drive 3.8 miles to gravel parking area with designated wheelchair accessible parking.

AMENITIES & FEES:

Vault toilet (wheelchair accessible), tables, grills, boat launch nearby. No fees for picnic area usage.

 Foot Note:

The Bois Brule has been known for over a hundred years as an exceptional trout fishing stream and has been fished by 5 Presidents of the U.S.: Grant, Cleveland, Coolidge, Hoover and Eisenhower (WI DNR 2002).

BARRIER BEACH PICNIC AREA*

Big Bay State Park, Madeline Island • Off WI 13, 78 miles from Superior, 20 miles from Ashland
*Gentle Hikes name

- **Appetizer: Take the Barrier Beach Almost Hike (pg. 168) for beach access and glorious views of Big Bay.**
- **Main Course: Tables are scattered on the grass throughout parking area as well as in open field.**
- **Dessert: Stroll close to the beach (sans the sand!) on the Boardwalk Interpretive Trail (pg. 120).**

PICNIC AREA DIRECTIONS & PARKING:

From Ferry Dock on Main Street turn right. Drive two blocks to Middle Road (note brown sign for Big Bay State Park); turn left. Travel 4 miles to stop sign (road name then changes to Hagen Road). Continue straight for 2 miles and turn left to park office. At first park stop sign turn right toward Campground, Picnic Area and Beach. At next stop sign turn right toward Picnic Area and

Beach, then left to Barrier Beach and paved parking lot. Wheelchair accessible parking, moped parking and bike racks available.

AMENITIES & FEES:
Vault toilets (wheelchair accessible), water, changing stalls, fire ring, benches, naturalist/environmental programs (see kiosk near blue shed for schedules). Annual or day use state park permit is required and is available at the park office.

BIG BAY POINT PICNIC AREA*

Big Bay State Park, Madeline Island • Off WI 13, 78 miles from Superior, 20 miles from Ashland
*Gentle Hikes name

- **Appetizer: Take the Big Bay Point Almost Hike (pg. 167) to a wonderful overlook as well as to scope out the best picnic table.**
- **Main Course: Tables are scattered about in a glorious old growth forest with many hemlocks 200–300 years old! This is wooded dining at its finest.**
- **Dessert: Your choice: Bay View Trail (pg. 118), which leads to beach access, or Point Trail/Loop (North) (pg. 114); both leave from this area.**

PICNIC AREA DIRECTIONS & PARKING:
From Ferry Dock on Main Street turn right. Drive two blocks to Middle Road (note brown sign indicating Big Bay State Park); turn left. Travel 4 miles to stop sign (road name then changes to Hagen Road). Continue straight for 2 miles and turn left to park office. At first park stop sign turn right toward Campground, Picnic Area and Beach. At next stop sign turn right toward Big Bay Point. Continue on road past Picnic Area and Beach to paved parking loop. Wheelchair accessible parking, moped parking and bike racks available.

AMENITIES & FEES:
Vault toilets (wheelchair accessible) 150' into trail, water. Annual or day use state park permit is required and is available at the park office.

BIG BAY TOWN PARK PICNIC AREA

Madeline Island • Off WI 13, 78 miles from Superior, 20 miles from Ashland

- **Appetizer: Take the Big Bay Town Park Lagoon Almost Hike (pg. 169) for spectacular views of the Big Bay Lagoon.**
- **Main Course: Tables in a semi-wooded setting for your dining pleasure.**
- **Dessert: Take the Big Bay Town Park Trail (pg. 128) for incredible Lake Superior and lagoon views as well as a wonderful beach area.**

PICNIC AREA DIRECTIONS & PARKING:
From Ferry Dock on Main Street turn left. Follow Main Street around right curve. It will become Big Bay Road and County Road H. At intersection with North Shore Road stay to right on County Road H. Continue past Black's

Shanty Road for 2 miles. Follow green sign for Big Bay Town Park. Turn right into Town Park and left to beach parking in sand and gravel lot. Designated wheelchair parking available.

AMENITIES & FEES:
Vault toilets (wheelchair accessible), water.

MEMORIAL PARK/JONI'S BEACH PICNIC AREA

Madeline Island • Off WI 13, 78 miles from Superior, 20 miles from Ashland

- **Appetizer: Take some time to read the dedications on benches and beautiful tribute to Joni.**
- **Main Course: Beachside tables serve up spectacular views of Lake Superior, the cliffs of the mainland shore and Bayfield marina.**
- **Dessert: This small area is big on scenery and worth coming back to for seconds!**

PICNIC AREA DIRECTIONS & PARKING:
From Ferry Dock on Main Street turn right and drive or walk 0.3 mile. Look for sign indicating Memorial Park, Joni's Beach on the lake side. Parking lot is paved.

AMENITIES & FEES:
Flush toilets (wheelchair accessible), water, grills, open-sided picnic shelter, small playground, boat launch, recycling facilities. No lifeguard at beach. No fees for picnic area use.

THOMPSON'S WEST END PICNIC AREA

Washburn • On WI 13, 91 miles from Superior, 7 miles from Ashland

- **Appetizer: Take the Not-to-be-Missed Panoramic Bay Stroll Almost Hike (pg. 170).**
- **Main Course: Many tables scattered about afford wonderful views of Chequamegon Bay and Lake Superior in the distance.**
- **Dessert: Wander out to the fishing pier or pick up a game of volleyball. This is a great park in which to spend some time.**

PICNIC AREA DIRECTIONS & PARKING:
From WI 13, turn south on 8th Avenue W toward Lake Superior. Drive 0.3 mile through residential neighborhood to gravel parking area.

AMENITIES & FEES:
Flush toilets (wheelchair accessible) in campground, water, grills, open-sided shelter, playground, volleyball net, fishing pier, boat launch. No lifeguard on duty at beach. No fees for trail use.

LONG LAKE PICNIC AREA

Chequamegon-Nicolet National Forest • Off WI 13, 93 miles from Superior, 5 miles from Ashland

- **Appetizer: Take the Long Lake Picnic Stroll Almost Hike (pg. 170) to scope out the best dining spot.**
- **Main Course: Wooded or lake view tables—your choice.**
- **Dessert: Long Lake Trail (pg. 146) beckons.**

PICNIC AREA DIRECTIONS & PARKING:

From WI 13 south of Washburn, turn west on Wanabo Road (various spellings, e.g., Wannebo, Wanabo, Wanebo). Travel 6 miles to sign for Chequamegon National Forest picnic grounds, Long Lake; turn right. Drive 0.1 mile to sign for Long Lake picnic grounds, boat landing; turn left and continue to paved parking area. Ample parking available with designated wheelchair accessible parking.

AMENITIES & FEES:

Vault toilets (wheelchair accessible), water, tables, grills, beach (no lifeguard). U.S. Forest vehicle stickers are required to park in this lot or day use fee of $3 (self-pay).

Long Lake Trail in Chequamegon-Nicolet National Forest (pg. 146). Photo by Melanie Morgan

Bowstring Bridge on the Amnicon Falls Geology Walk (pg. 56). Photo by Melanie Morgan

HIKING FOR HEALTH

Tyler Forks at Copper Falls State Park (Three Bridges Trail pg. 94). Photo by Ladona Tornabene

INCREDIBLE STUFF EVEN WE COULDN'T MAKE UP!

It's been said that if the beneficial effects of exercise could be put into pill form, it would easily be a trillion dollar seller!

The health benefits of walking/hiking are phenomenal! These benefits extend beyond the obvious physical component of health. They encompass the psychological (mental and emotional), social and spiritual components of health as well.

Let's begin by taking a quick glance at the physical health of our nation. Let's look at the cons of being inactive as well as the pros of being active so that you don't have to become one of the nation's statistics.

Drawbacks of Inactivity and Benefits of Physical Activity

Physical inactivity alone is responsible for over a quarter million deaths in this country every year according to the Centers for Disease Control.[1]

Physical activity will reduce the risk of death due to inactivity.[2]

Heart disease is the number one killer of both men and women in this nation.

Exercise such as walking or hiking can prevent heart attacks and heart disease for both men and women.[3,4]

It has been known for a long time that inactive people have nearly twice the risk of developing heart disease as active people.[5]

Walking briskly for 5 or more hours per week can reduce the risk of heart attack by 50%.[3]

Cancer is the second leading cause of death among Americans.

Walking can reduce the risk of some cancers by 50%.[6]

Stroke is the third leading cause of death; high blood pressure is a major risk factor for strokes.

Physical activity such as walking can not only prevent and reduce the high blood pressure that leads to strokes, it can also prevent the strokes as well.[7,8]

High cholesterol is a risk factor for strokes, heart disease and heart attacks.

One study showed that walking could improve cholesterol ratios and reduce heart disease risk whether one walked fast or slow.[9]

Listed above are just some of the drawbacks of inactivity and the benefits of physical activity. Want to know more? Read on.

The Battle of the Bulge: "Figuring" it Out

Overweight and obesity are continuing at epidemic levels in the U.S. according to researchers published in the Journal of the American Medical Association.[10]

Nearly two thirds of American adults are overweight—a percentage that affects more than just one figure as the yearly cost of overweight and obesity was estimated to be nearly $122.9 billion.[11] This figure is comparable to the economic costs of cigarette smoking![11]

Potential Casualties

People who are obese have a 50–100% risk of death from all causes compared to that of individuals who are not overweight.[11] Overweight and obesity are known risk factors for diabetes, heart disease, stroke, hypertension, gall bladder disease, osteoarthritis, breathing disorders such as sleep apnea and some cancers.[11] The risks for diabetes increase with weight gain.[12,13] For the first time, overweight and obesity were directly linked with increasing the risk of heart failure.[14] The largest study ever done on excess weight and cancer has linked increased body weight with higher death rates from several different cancers (breast, colorectal, esophageal, gallbladder, kidney, pancreatic, prostate, uterine and many others).[15]

Battle Plan

Researchers from a National Institute of Health study concluded that reduced amounts of physical activity may be the most important current factor explaining the rising prevalence of obesity in the United States.[16] Exercise such as walking has, by itself, been an effective method for reducing weight.[2] Walking can help with weight loss as it burns about 100 calories per mile depending upon body weight (hiking can burn more).[17] Walking also helps shed fat while keeping muscle, which is good because muscle actually helps burn calories. Studies have also demonstrated that exercise can induce a short term decrease in appetite for most people.[18] One study found that weight loss over time was associated with decreased risk for type 2 diabetes.[13] Another study discovered that for every 2000 calories burned during leisure time activities, the rate of diabetes was reduced by 24%.[12] Other studies have demonstrated that the benefits of walking include the prevention and control of diabetes.[6,19,12]

A researcher at Harvard was quoted as saying, "Avoiding weight gain, along with not smoking, is one of the most important things people can do to protect their long term health."[20,21] Walking is one of the most effective methods for maintaining weight loss over time.[2]

Victory!

The above studies are a testament to the health benefits of adopting and maintaining a physically active lifestyle. This guide may help you as the benefits obtained from walking are transferable to hiking. Hiking is actually considered to be more vigorous than walking, even when traveling at the same speed.[17] This is due to probable trail surface conditions such as rocks, roots, gravel and varying terrain as well as environmental factors.

The "Golden Standard" for maximizing the physical benefits derived from exercise is 30 minutes or more of moderate-intensity physical activity most days of the week.[22] Intensity should be performed at a pace faster than a stroll but slow enough to engage in conversation. To meet this criteria, look to our trails between 1 and 1.5 miles with the rating. Even if you aren't able to achieve the "Golden Standard" right away, any amount of physical activity is important and can have beneficial effects. As a matter of fact, a recent study stated that walking for 5 minutes at a time, 6 times per day, on most days of the week can improve heart health for inactive people.[23] For shorter walks, look to our Almost Hikes that range from 90' to just under a half-mile. Even if you cannot get to any of these trails, the key is to add movement to your life in whatever ways that you can. Start slowly, be comfortable and make it fun!

More victorious news!

Walking helps prevent and reduce debilitating problems such as back pain and osteoporosis. Brisk walking has also been shown to strengthen the immune system and help fight stress thus potentially preventing colds, flus and other infections.[19,24] Furthermore, exercise increases energy levels for several hours after completing the activity.[25,26] But keep in mind that health is more than just physical.

Psychological Benefits of Walking/Hiking

Many people are unaware that the simple act of walking or hiking can provide a multitude of psychological benefits beyond the expected physical ones. It has been shown that:

Exercise is linked to a reduction of stress and an increase in energy.

Exercise can be used for prevention and treatment of mild to moderate depression.

Exercise is associated with reductions in everyday anxiety as well as anxiety disorders.

Exercise has beneficial emotional effects across all ages and in both sexes.

Exercise improves physical fitness, which can lead to better mental health, increased self esteem and greater feelings of well-being and positive emotion.[25,18,27,28,26]

Newer research reveals that exercise can help the cognitive functioning of the brain. In other words, people are able to think better because they exercise.[29] This increase in cognitive functioning with exercise extends all the way into and throughout the aging process (beyond 80 years old).[30] Other research showed that walking also reduced the risk of memory loss or the decline of mental functioning that occurs with age. Their recommendation: Walk a mile or more per day.[31] One study showed that aerobic exercise such as walking resulted in a decrease in brain tissue loss due to age.[32]

All ages can benefit from exercise. There is a strong relationship among children who exercise, faster learning and better retention of information.[33]

Another interesting finding is that exercise has been shown to reduce cravings for cigarettes while trying to quit and to decrease the likelihood of smoking.[34,18]

For better health on the inside—get outside!

Hiking outdoors produces many benefits for mental health that go beyond the effects of the exercise itself. Simply being in the outdoors adds a sense of calm and peace.[35] Actually, just looking at the color green has been shown to have a calming effect.[36,37]

Social Benefits of Walking/Hiking

Many therapists utilize outdoor pursuits to effect changes in interpersonal relationships. Hiking may be more of a social activity than walking. Most people take along another person or more when venturing out for a hike for safety as well as other reasons. Additionally, people often want to share the special beauty, sights and sounds of the outdoors with someone. There are no TVs blaring, no phones ringing (leave the cell phone off!), no chores calling while outside. New terrain to explore and discuss gives additional advantage to hiking. Couples and friends can improve their relationships by talking while walking. In one study, couples found themselves growing closer because of the additional time spent together without competing distractions.[38]

So, grab a friend and/or loved one to share a trail with you. But please remember that others on the trail may be seeking solitude or a spiritual experience. Therefore, keep conversation volume down as voices travel a long way in the woods, especially near water.

Spiritual Benefits of Walking/Hiking

There is no question that being out in nature can awaken a deep part of us like nothing else can. For many people, walking in the woods or other natural settings can help them to realize or even access feelings of spirituality in ways not possible through other methods. A recent article found that people often use such recreational activities as camping, canoeing, walking or riding in wooded areas, and even gardening to connect to their inner spirituality.[39] It seems that natural environments serve as a type of connection to spiritual experience.[35] Appreciating the world's natural beauty has been a part of most spiritual traditions from the very beginning of time. Since time is at such a premium in most people's lives, it has been suggested to use exercise time (walking, running, hiking, etc.) to commune with God or to pray.[40] Many people find an enormous sense of peace or an enlarging of the soul where time seems to slow down, and problems seem to drift away.

Until our paths meet again...

It is the authors' hope that all of this information will encourage you to get out and explore the trails in this guide. But don't wait until you are near the South Shore of Lake Superior to hike. Explore local trails and neighborhood parks. Start or join a walking/hiking club in your own community. Treat yourself to a mental workout by reading other reputable health and fitness books (see Appendix A for suggestions).

Remember the steps you take toward a healthy lifestyle today will eventually create a path to that same destination. Healthy trails to you—however you travel them.

Note: The information presented herein is in NO way intended to substitute for medical advice. It is best to seek medical advice from a reputable medical professional. For your maximum well-being, we strongly recommend getting your doctor's approval before beginning any physical activity program.

Memorial Park Wayside (pg. 176). This view is wheelchair accessible and may also be seen from your vehicle. Photo by Melanie Morgan

FOR TRAVELERS WITH SPECIFIC NEEDS

Copper Falls on Three Bridges Trail (pg. 94; picnic area pg. 191). Three Bridges Trail has two sections that meet Universal Design Standards, one of which offers an unprecedented view of Copper Falls for persons using wheelchairs. Photo by Ladona Tornabene

FOR OUR READERS WITH PHYSICAL CHALLENGES

This chapter contains information about features on trails, Almost Hikes, picnic areas and waysides that are designed for persons with disabilities. For more general information about trails, Almost Hikes, picnic areas and waysides, please see their respective sections.

A Candid Message

After hearing the true story of a man who took his wife (in a wheelchair) on a trail that contained over 300 steps (spread throughout) and inclines at 36% grade—we had to pause and reflect on what we say regarding accessibility. While we are hesitant to label hikes as accessible or not, we do aspire to present the trails in our book with honesty, integrity and straightforwardness. As we reviewed the Regulatory Negotiation Committee on Accessibility Guidelines for Outdoor Developed Areas (Final Report, September 30, 1999), we knew we were not qualified to assess our trails according to these standards, nor have we attempted to do so. Although a few of our trails may meet Universal Design Standards, we only indicate those the state parks or other entities claim as officially meeting such standards. See the "Flattest Trails" list below.

For the remainder of trails in this book, we have developed our own rating criteria (see pg. 20). We note those things that may present challenges (e.g. inclines, rocks, roots, steps, etc.) as well as those features that may be helpful (i.e. benches, handrails, paved trails, etc.). On each trail we stated total trail length, trail surface, average tread width, total number of inclines and the steepest and longest (exceeding 30') incline. We report all inclines exceeding 10 degrees (18% grade). We used a clinometer to measure the inclines (running slope, not cross-slope) and chose to report in degrees rather than % grade (see Appendix C for conversion chart).

We put significant detail on each trail so our readers would know the locations (rounded to tenths of a mile) of various features. This way each person could make an informed decision based on his/her abilities as to how far to go on a certain trail or whether to choose another altogether.

Inclines on the Trails

On all of our trails, we report inclines. If a trail states that there are no inclines exceeding 10 degrees (18% grade), it does not necessarily mean that it is flat. The trail could (and often does) have inclines of lesser degrees. To alert our readers to the flattest trails (flattest defined by what our naked eye could perceive), we formed a list also displayed in Authors' Corner, but reformatted here for your convenience.

Flattest Trails

Superior

Additional Information About the Flattest Trails

SUPERIOR: The Millennium Trail East and West (p. 24–27) is a new trail with an extremely smooth, wide blacktop surface. It is the only paved trail to run through the second-to-largest municipal forest located within a city in the United States. It has been constructed to meet the standards for Universal Design.

Riverfront Trail (pg. 28) is paved and predominately flat; however, access points are not. We were told by Parks and Recreation that persons with valid hang-tags or license plates indicating mobility impairments are permitted to park at the N. 21st Street Boat Launch. Travel west to the end of N. 21st Street and find an access road that leads down to the boat launch and trail access. This entry point is flat.

Barker's Island Trail (pg. 30) is completely paved and relatively flat.

Sections of the Osaugie Trail featured in this book are mostly paved multi-use paths; however, some sections have gravel and involve active railroad crossings. The flattest, completely paved sections are Superior Bay to Trail Beginning (pg. 32) and Superior Bay to Old Stockade Site (pg. 36) with the exception of some very gradual inclines. Also, asphalt may be uneven in places.

The Dog Trail (pg. 52) at Pattison State Park averages 6–8' wide with three different surfaces: grass, hardpacked dirt and gravel. It may be uneven in places as well as have standing water at certain times, but made our Best Wooded Trail category. Trailhead may be difficult to locate and requires driving through the campground.

Rhonda & Joe's Wedding Stroll Almost Hike (pg. 152) is actually a sidewalk that runs through the park and the grassy area is flat, fairly even and was used by someone in a wheelchair for the wedding. Another point of interest is the playground that is accessible with a portable toilet that is also wheelchair accessible.

Welcome-A-Board-Walk Almost Hike (pg. 152) is actually boardwalk that is wide and flat but uneven in places. Exhibit area to SS *Meteor* is accessible, but not the ship.

The Superior Entry Almost Hike (pg. 154) is paved and flat. The parking area has some packed and some loose gravel, but is very close to trailhead. Once on the path, the first 200' of sidewalk en route to the pier is nearly flawless; however, just prior to the pier is a gouge in the pavement. This area may be bypassed depending on size and style of wheelchair. After that, the cement pier is very smooth and 30' wide.

Big Manitou Falls Almost Hike (pg. 155) has a paved parking area with designated wheelchair accessible space but involves crossing a county road. The remainder of the path is about 4' wide and paved but very uneven due to tree root protrusions. The 10° decline just preceding the falls becomes an incline on the return but can be completely bypassed by taking the paved trail (plowed in the winter) around the picnic area. However, that route is also uneven due to tree root protrusions. Worth the trek? We think so as Big Manitou Falls is the highest in the state and is striking, especially during periods of high water flow! It made our Best Waterfalls category.

The Amnicon Falls Wooded and Riverview Stroll Almost Hike (pg. 158) offers a very wide, level grassy section starting from the designated wheelchair accessible picnic area up to the open-sided picnic shelter. This is a short but nice wooded section.

ASHLAND: All of the trails at The Northern Great Lakes Visitor Center meet Universal Design Standards. The Boardwalk Trail East Loop (pg. 72) and West Loop (pg. 74) have selected paved entry points. Though these points are not completely flat (declines initially, but inclines on the return), access is eased by paved surface. The remainder of the trail is flat and consists of hardpacked gravel and boardwalk. The Northern Great Lakes Visitor Center Indoor Outing (Almost Hike) is a unique experience and our first ever indoor hike! Our description of this Almost Hike (pg. 159) contains stairs; however, there is elevator access to those same displays. Just stop at 2nd floor and Mezzanine Level, which are both accessible. This visitor center (VC) is truly remarkable. If you go, we highly recommend spending some time there as it is not your typical VC. The entire facility is barrier-free.

The entire Ashland Bayfront Trail (p. 82–93) is a mostly paved multi-use path; however, some sections have stairs. The section from Maslowski Beach to Hot Pond (pg. 82) is reasonably flat and paved but crosses a parking lot, entry drives and does allow vehicles on part of the trail en route to a fishing spot. The trail also passes literally within feet of busy U.S. 2. Although plans are in the making to re-route U.S. 2, construction had not begun at time of writing (summer 2003). The paved and flat section from Hot Pond to Reiss Coal Dock (pg. 86) is situated well off U.S. 2. Another flat portion is located within the Memorial Park to Krehar Park section and is best accessed from the Ellis Avenue off U.S. 2. Ellis Avenue borders the Chequamegon Hotel and leads to the Ashland marina. A wheelchair designated parking space is near the quaint gazebo. It is 75' from the parking space to the gazebo and picnic table. All sections made our Best Lake Superior View list.

Prentice Park Promenade East and West Almost Hikes (p. 160–161) offer wide grassy surfaces that may be slightly uneven in places. They are also multi-use trails, but ATVs are not permitted. The Prentice Park Wooded Stroll Almost Hike (pg. 160) is not as wide but is reasonably flat and offers a more secluded feel.

COPPER FALLS STATE PARK: The Three Bridges Trail (pg. 94) at Copper Falls State Park has two sections that meet Universal Design Standards and feature Copper Falls, Brownstone Falls, the Bad River and a section of the North Country National Scenic Trail. Although part of the main trail, these sections have separate entry points that require valid hang-tags or plates. If you do not have such identification and need to use these entry points, stop at the park office so that accommodations may be made. Please do not take RVs or trailers to these lots as there is not enough space to turn around. Follow trailhead directions on pg. 94 and turn right at Access Road marked "Wheelchairs Only" located 1.2 miles beyond park office. Follow the accessibility signs from the park road to a gravel lot designated wheelchair accessible. Vault toilets at trailhead are not accessible as of Spring 2004, but plans are underway for renovation. However, flush toilets at park office or gift shop/concessions are accessible (see Copper Falls Picnic Area pg. 191).

To access Copper and Brownstone Falls (0.5 mile total trail length), begin from northwest corner of parking area to the left. Expect gravel and hardpacked dirt surface; 8–10' wide. Follow accessibility signs. In 100' find overlook of Brownstone Falls where it plummets into the Bad River gorge. Interpretive sign reveals more information about the history of this gorge. Continue on this path along a nice wooded trail. At trail intersection, turn left. This section bypasses a steep grade on the main trail. Where path rejoins main trail, turn left. Soon you will encounter a wide bridge with a spectacular view of Copper Falls! This is noteworthy because the spring of 2004 is the first season that Copper Falls became accessible to persons using wheelchairs. Spend some time here enjoying the view then retrace path to trailhead.

To follow sections of the North Country National Scenic Trail as it parallels the Bad River (0.4 mile total trail length), begin from northeast corner of parking area to the right. Expect gravel and hardpacked dirt surface; 5–6' wide. Follow accessibility signs. Pass vault toilets. At trail intersection, turn right. Path parallels Bad River. Alert: Steep dropoffs on river side of trail. At trail intersection, turn left and cross bridge (wood, double handrail). Views abound up- and down-river. At end of bridge, turn left. Accessible portion of path continues for approximately another 400' along the Bad River. You will see a sign indicating end of accessible trail. Retrace path to trailhead.

The Loon Lake Beach Area Almost Hike (pg. 162) also meets Universal Design Standards and provides direct access to the water at Loon Lake Beach Area.

CHEQUAMEGON-NICOLET NATIONAL FOREST: Chequamegon-Nicolet National Forest is planning to have Morgan Falls (pg. 102) meet Universal Design Standards. At time of writing (June 2003) there were no benches and trail narrowed to 3' in places.

MADELINE ISLAND: Point Trail/Loops South and North (p. 110–117) are hardpacked dirt/gravel and average 2–4' wide. They are basically flat but somewhat uneven in places, as is the Big Bay Point Almost Hike (pg. 167). The Big Bay Town Park Lagoon Almost Hike (pg. 169) is flat and primarily on hardpacked sand, but can be somewhat soft when wet.

The Boardwalk Interpretive Trail (pg. 120) can be accessed from a paved parking area, then onto a wide grassy surface that leads to hardpacked dirt, asphalt and eventually, boardwalk. It is basically flat with the exception of one paved decline between 8–10° en route to boardwalk, which becomes an incline on the return.

All of these Madeline Island trails received our Best Lake Superior View rating in Authors' Corner (pg. 12) with the exception of Big Bay Town Park Lagoon, which received Best Vista rating. Point Trail/Loops and Big Bay Point Almost Hike made Best Wooded category as well.

BAYFIELD: Brownstone Trail North (pg. 138) has sections of soft sand. There were two areas of erosion on this trail at time of writing (June 2003).

WASHBURN: Washburn Walking Trail (wheelchair accessible section, pg. 144) is a hardpacked gravel trail that is officially designated by symbol as being wheelchair accessible. However, it is not slated as meeting Universal Design Standards.

For a complete listing of all paved trails and shortest trails, refer to the Authors' Corner on pg. 12. Please note that most of our Almost Hikes are under 0.5 mile in total length.

Restroom Accessibility

Please refer to individual Trail, Almost Hike, Wayside and Picnic Area descriptions throughout this book.

Waysides and Picnic Areas

We created charts in order to feature those waysides and picnic areas that have one or more accessible features. To assist those who need specific information on wheelchair accessibility, we indicate designated parking spaces and other facts that may be helpful. Since this chart is not a comprehensive listing of all the waysides and picnic areas in this book, please refer to their individual descriptions.

At Siskiwit Bay Park & Wayside, there was a 3–5" concrete step to deck surface at picnic shelter. Same condition for bench access.

Note: Although not listed on the charts, Penokee Scenic Overlook (pg. 161) has picnic table with extension, grills, vault toilet (wheelchair accessible). At time of writing (June 2003), access to toilet was under construction. The Overlook is not visible from the picnic area and boardwalk to overlook has 83 steps (non-continuous).

Historical Marker of the Bad River (pg. 177) and Gogebic Wayside (pg. 177) have informational markers that can be read from your vehicle.

When Snowflakes Fly

No paved trails are plowed in the winter unless otherwise noted in this chapter.

RESOURCES
Open the Outdoors: Accessible Recreation Opportunities

"Open the Outdoors" is a nationwide effort to provide disabled individuals with a user-friendly means of accessing recreation opportunities.

The Wisconsin Department of Natural Resources is committed to providing greater access and more programs for persons with disabilities.

For more information on accessibility, contact:

Dotti Krieger
DNR Accessibility Coordinator
608-267-7490

These waysides have one or more accessible features.

WAYSIDE/SCENIC LOCALE	PAGE NUMBER	RESTROOM TYPE	RESTROOM ACCESSIBLE	SURFACE TO RESTROOM	SURFACE TO TABLES	SURFACE UNDER TABLE	TABLE EXTENSION	DESIGNATED PARKING	VIEWS FROM CAR	VISTOR CENTER
Old Stockade Site	174				Paved	Paved		X	X	
Northwest Portal of Wisconsin (Superior)	175	Flush	X	Paved	Grass	Grass		X		X
Brule River	175	Vault	X	Paved	Grass	Grass	X	X		
Iron River	175	Vault	X	Paved	Paved, grass	Grass	X	X	X	
Overlook Park	176				Grass, paved	Grass, decking		X	X	
Memorial Park	176				Grass	Grass		X	X	
Wisconsin Travel Info Center (Hurley)	178	Flush	X	Paved	Paved	Paved	X	X		X
Jardine Creek	179	Vault	X	Paved	Paved, grass	Paved, grass	X	X	X	
Siskiwit Bay	179	Flush	X	Paved	Grass	Paved, grass		X	X	

These picnic areas have one or more accessible features.

PICNIC AREA	PAGE NUMBER	SURFACE TO TABLES	SURFACE UNDER TABLE	ACCESSIBLE TABLE	RESTROOM TYPE	RESTROOM ACCESSIBLE	SURFACE TO RESTROOM	DESIGNATED PARKING
Barker's Island	184	Paved	Paved	X				X
Barker's Island Play Area	184	Grass	Grass	X	Portable	X	Paved	Nearby
Billings Park	185	Grass	Grass	X	Flush	X	Paved	X
Bear Creek Park	185	Paved	Paved		Portable			
Big Manitou Falls	186	Grass	Grass		Vault		Paved	X
Pattison State Park Main	186	Paved, grass	Paved, grass	X	Flush	X	Paved	X
Little Manitou Falls	187	Grass	Grass		Vault		Grass	X
Amnicon (Sheltered)	188	Paved, grass	Paved, grass					Spr 2004
Amnicon (Accessible)	188	Paved	Paved	X	Vault	X	Paved	X
Bois Brule	189	Grass	Grass	X				X
Prentice Park	189	Paved, grass	Paved, grass	X	Flush	X	Paved	X
Maslowski Beach	190	Paved	Paved	X	Flush	X	Paved	X
Krehar Park	190	Paved, grass	Paved, grass	X	Flush	X	Paved	X
Copper Falls Park Main	191	Grass	Grass	X	Flush	X	Stone	X
Bayview Park	191	Paved, grass	Paved, grass	X	Flush	X	Paved	X
Saxon Harbor	192	Paved	Paved	X	Vault	X	Paved	
Mouth of the Brule River	193	Grass	Grass	X	Vault	X	Paved	X
Barrier Beach	193	Grass	Grass	X	Vault	X	Paved	X
Big Bay Point	194	Grass	Grass	X	Vault	X	Gravel, paved	X
Big Bay Town Park	194	Grass	Grass	X	Vault	X	Paved	X
Memorial Park/Joni's Beach	195	Grass	Grass/sand		Flush	X	Paved	
Thompson's West End	195	Grass	Grass		Flush	X	Paved	
Long Lake	196	Paved, grass	Paved, grass	X	Vault	X	Paved	X

FOR OUR READERS TRAVELING IN RVS

This chapter summarizes some of the information included throughout this book regarding state parks, trails, Almost Hikes, waysides and picnic areas that may be of assistance to our readers traveling in RVs. For a full description of each of the trails, Almost Hikes, waysides and picnic areas, please see their respective chapters.

State and local parks

The following have designated RV parking spaces within a lot shared with other vehicles: Pattison State Park (Main picnic area), Prentice Park (Main picnic area).

When visiting Amnicon Falls State Park, turn left at first stop sign then take a right and travel over bridge. Parking is available near open-sided shelter or at the next right in paved lot. RV access and pull-through capabilities will be determined by how vehicles are positioned in these parking areas. The reason the park does not recommend that RVs drive to the covered bridge is due to a very narrow one-way street and tight turn-around in the respective parking area.

Trails

Parking areas for the following trails have designated RV spaces:

Note: For access to all trails at Amnicon Falls State Park (e.g. Geology Walk, pg. 56; Picnic Stroll, pg. 60; Thimbleberry Nature Trail, pg. 62), turn left at first stop sign, then take a right and travel over bridge. Parking is available near open-sided shelter or at the next right in paved lot.

The Ashland Bayfront Trail passes through Krehar Park (pg. 88), which is a designated RV campground (no tents). Although there are no fees for picnic area/trail usage, there is a $20 fee per day for campground (self-pay).

Almost Hikes

Parking areas for the following Almost Hikes have designated RV spaces:

Waysides & Scenic Locales

While we encourage you to read through our detailed descriptions of the waysides and scenic locales starting on pg. 172, for your convenience we have included here those that have designated RV parking and highway pull-throughs (plus we tell you other information at a glance that may be helpful). We have listed them in chart format (pg. 216) for your convenience and state the following information:

Designated parking: Indicates that there are spaces specifically designed to accommodate RVs.

Highway pull-through: A designated area with an easy exit off the highway and an easy entrance back onto the highway. Since there are no designated parking places, RV access and pull-through capabilities will be determined by how vehicles are positioned.

Type of restroom: Indicates toilet type—flush (modern), vault (pit), portable (port-a-pottys, portalets).

Picnic tables: Ideal for a quick lunch when traveling, but do check out our entire 'spread' on picnic areas (pg. 182).

Visitor center: Indicates if there is a center at the site or nearby.

Also, many of the waysides are closed during snow season as they are not plowed.

Picnic Areas

While we encourage you to read through our detailed descriptions of the picnic areas in this book starting on pg. 182, for your convenience we have included here those that have designated RV parking.

These as well as all picnic areas featured in this book have a knack for working up an appetite for scenic beauty. Bon appetit!

These waysides and scenic locales have features useful for those traveling in RVs.

WAYSIDE/SCENIC LOCALE	PAGE NUMBER	RV PARKING	HWY PULL-THROUGH	RESTROOM TYPE	PICNIC TABLES	VISITOR CENTER
Northwest Portal of Wisconsin (Superior)	175	X	X	Flush	X	X
Brule River	175	X	X	Vault	X	
Iron River	175	X	X	Vault	X	
Overlook Park	176		X		X	
Memorial Park	176		X		Nearby	
Historical Marker of the Bad River	177		X			
Gogebic Iron Range	177	X	X		X	
WI Travel Info Center (Hurley)	178	X	X	Flush	X	X
Jardine Creek	179		X	Vault	X	
Siskiwit Bay Park	179		X	Flush	X	

APPENDICES

Upson Falls (pg. 163). Photo by Ladona Tornabene

APPENDIX A: RECOMMENDED READINGS, RESOURCES AND REFERENCES

The following are recommended resources for your health and enjoyment.

Hiking Wisconsin

Chequamegon-Nicolet National Forest, Forest Service and United States Department of Agriculture. *Trails in the Chequamegon: A Guide to Trails.* [Booklet], 2003.

Forest Service, Nicolet National Forest. *Trails of Nicolet National Forest: A Guide to Trails in the Nicolet National Forest.* [Booklet], 2003.

Hansen, E. *Hiking Wisconsin: A Falcon Guide.* Guilford, CT: The Globe Pequot Press, 2002.

Hintz, M. *Hiking Wisconsin: America's Best Day Hiking Series.* Champaign, IL: Human Kinetics, 1997.

Lisi, P. *Wisconsin Waterfalls: A Touring Guide.* Black Earth, WI: Prairie Oak Press, 2000.

McGrath, W.C. *Great Wisconsin Walks: 45 Strolls, Rambles, Hikes, and Treks.* Black Earth, WI: Trails Books, 1997.

Hiking Minnesota's North Shore

Slade, A. (Ed.). *Guide to the Superior Hiking Trail.* Two Harbors, MN: Ridgeline Press, 2001.

Tornabene, L., M. Morgan and L. Vogelsang. *Gentle Hikes: Minnesota's Most Scenic North Shore Hikes Under 3 Miles.* Cambridge, MN: Adventure Publications, Inc., 2002.

State Parks

Bailey, B. *Wisconsin State Parks, State Forests and Recreation Areas.* Saginaw, MI: Glovebox Guidebooks of America, 2000.

Field Guides

Lein, K. *Ferns of Big Bay State Park.* [Brochure] Wisconsin Department of Natural Resources, 1995.

Moyle, J. and E. Moyle. *Northland Wildflowers: The Comprehensive Guide to the Minnesota Region.* Minneapolis: University of Minnesota Press, 2001.

Oslund, C. and M. Oslund. *What's Doin' the Bloomin'?* Duluth: Plant Pics LLP, 2001.

Tekiela, S. *Birds of Wisconsin Field Guide.* Cambridge, MN: Adventure Publications, Inc., 1999.

Tekiela, S. *Reptiles & Amphibians of Wisconsin Field Guide.* Cambridge, MN: Adventure Publications, Inc., 2004.

Tekiela, S. *Trees of Wisconsin Field Guide.* Cambridge, MN: Adventure Publications, Inc., 2002.

Tekiela, S. *Wildflowers of Wisconsin Field Guide.* Cambridge, MN: Adventure Publications, Inc., 2000.

Family Fun

Shanberg, K. and S. Tekiela. *Plantworks: A Wild Plant Cookbook, Field Guide and Activity Book*. Cambridge, MN: Adventure Publications, Inc., 1991.

Tekiela, S. and K. Shanberg. *Nature Smart: A Family Guide to Nature*. Cambridge, MN: Adventure Publications, Inc., 1995.

Tekiela, S. and K. Shanberg. *Start Mushrooming: The Easiest Way to Start Collecting 6 Edible Mushrooms*. Cambridge, MN: Adventure Publications, Inc., 1993.

Health and Wellness

Alsbro, D. *The Best Little Book of Wellness*. Benton Harbor, MI: Rainbow Wellness, 2000.

Cooper, K. *Faith-Based Fitness*. Nashville, TN: Thomas Nelson Publishers, 1997.

Leith, L.M. *Exercising Your Way to Better Mental Health*. Morgantown, WV: Fitness Information Technology, 1998.

Walking

Sweetgall, R. *Walk the Four Seasons: Walking and Cross-training Logbook*. Clayton, MO: Creative Walking, Inc., 1992.

Stretching

Anderson, B. and J. Anderson. *Stretching (Revised)*. Berkeley, CA: Publishers Group West, 2000.

Additional Resources, Including Websites

North Country Trail Association
National Headquarters
229 East Main Street
Lowell, MI 49331
888-454-NCTA or www.northcountrytrail.org
email: hq@northcountrytrail.org

Vacation Planning

Ashland Chamber of Commerce & County Tourism
P.O. Box 746
805 Lake Shore Drive West
Ashland, WI 54806
1-800-284-9484 or www.travelashland.com

Bayfield Chamber of Commerce
P.O. Box 138
Bayfield, WI 54814
1-800-447-4094 or www.bayfield.org

Bayfield County Tourism & Recreation
P.O. Box 832
117 East 6th Street
Washburn, WI 54891
1-800-472-6338 or www.travelbayfield.com

Hurley Area Chamber of Commerce
316 Silver Street
Hurley, WI 54534
(715) 561-4334 or www.HurleyWi.com

24 hour winter snow & recreation reports: (715) 561-3866

Northern Great Lakes Visitor Center
29270 County Highway G
Ashland, WI 54806
(715) 685-9983 or www.northerngreatlakescenter.org

Superior-Douglas County Visitor Center
305 Harbor View Parkway
Superior, WI 54880
1-800-942-5313 ext. 21 or www.visitsuperior.com

Want to help improve the quality of outdoor experiences for everyone?
Consider becoming a Friend of Wisconsin State Parks, a nonprofit partnership
organized to enhance, preserve, protect and promote Wisconsin state parks,
forests, trails and recreation areas. Contact Friends of Wisconsin State Parks,
P.O. Box 2271, Madison, WI 53701.

APPENDIX B: TRAIL HEADQUARTERS INFORMATION

The following is atopic-specific list of phone numbers, addresses and applicable websites of all trail headquarters pertaining to the trails featured in this book.

A common phone number and website for all Wisconsin state parks is the Department of Natural Resources (1-608-266-2621, www.dnr.wi.gov), but for specific information, contact the individual parks.

State Parks

Amnicon Falls State Park
c/o 6294 South State Road 35
Superior, WI 54880-8326
Winter: (715) 399-3111; Summer: (715) 398-3000
www.dnr.state.wi.us/org/land/parks/specific/amnicon

Big Bay State Park
Box 589
Bayfield, WI 54814-0589
(715) 747-6425
www.dnr.state.wi.us/org/land/parks/specific/bigbay

Copper Falls State Park
Route 1, Box 17AA
Mellen, WI 54546
(715) 274-5123
www.dnr.state.wi.us/org/land/parks/specific/copperfalls

Pattison State Park
6294 South State Road 35
Superior, WI 54880-8326
(715) 399-3111
www.dnr.state.wi.us/org/land/parks/specific/pattison/
email: Kerry.Isensee@dnr.state.wi.us (Information)

Chambers of Commerce and Visitor Centers

Ashland Chamber of Commerce & County Tourism
P.O. Box 746
805 Lake Shore Drive West
Ashland, WI 54806
1-800-284-9484 or www.travelashland.com

Bayfield Chamber of Commerce
P.O. Box 138
Bayfield, WI 54814
1-800-447-4094 or www.bayfield.org

Madeline Island Chamber of Commerce
P.O. Box 274
274 Middle Road
La Pointe, WI 54850
1-888-475-3386 or (715) 747-2801 or www.madelineisland.com

Northern Great Lakes Visitor Center
29270 County Highway G
Ashland, WI 54806
(715) 685-9983 or www.northerngreatlakescenter.org

Superior-Douglas County Visitor Center
305 Harbor View Parkway
Superior, WI 54880
1-800-942-5313, ext. 21 or www.visitsuperior.com

State and National Forests

Brule River State Forest
6250 South Ranger Road
P.O. Box 125
Brule, WI 54820-0125
(715) 372-5678 or
www.dnr.wi.gov/org/land/Forestry/StateForests/meet.htm#BruleR

Chequamegon-Nicolet National Forest
Forest Supervisor's Office
1170 4th Avenue South
Park Falls, WI 54552
(715) 762-2461
(715) 762-5701 (TTY)
(715) 762-5179 (fax)

Chequamegon-Nicolet National Forest
Great Divide Ranger District
Glidden Office
P.O. Box 128
Highway 13 North
Glidden, WI 54527
(715) 264-2511 (voice & TTY) or (715) 264-3307

Washburn Ranger District
P.O. Box 578
113 Bayfield Street
Washburn, WI 54891
(715) 373-2667
(715) 373-2878 (TTY)
(715) 373 2878 (fax)

DNR Service Center Locations

Ashland
DNR Service Center
2501 Golf Course Road
Ashland, WI 54806
(715) 685-2900
(715) 685-2909 (fax)

Central Office
101 South Webster Street
Madison, WI 53703
(608) 266-2621
(608) 261-4380 (fax)
(608) 267-6897 (TDD)

Superior
DNR Service Center
1401 Tower Avenue
Superior, WI 54880
(715) 392-7988
(715) 392-7993 (fax)

North Country Trail

North Country Trail Association (NCTA)
National Headquarters
229 East Main Street
Lowell, MI 49331
888-454-NCTA or www.northcountrytrail.org
email: hq@northcountrytrail.org

NCTA Great Lakes Trail Council
Wisconsin Coordinator:
Brad Gingras
P.O. Box 416
Cable, WI 54821-0416
715-798-3890
email: nctrail@cablemuseum.org

Other

Bayfield Winery Ltd. (Hauser's)
86565 County Trunk J
Bayfield, WI 54814
(715) 779-5404

Iron County Development Zone Council
P.O. Box 97-IT
100 Cary Road
Hurley, WI 54534
715-561-2922
email: ironctydev@gogebic.cc.wi.us

Superior Parks and Recreation
1316 North 14th Street
Superior, WI 54880
(715) 395-7270 or www.ci.superior.wi.us

APPENDIX C: TECHNICAL SPECIFICATIONS

Forgive us, but remember that two of us are professors and the other—a former accountant!

Measuring distances

All trails were rolled with a Rolotape (400 series—professional). Distances were recorded in feet, then rounded to the nearest tenth of a mile.

Measuring inclines

Inclines were measured with a clinometer (Suunto MC-2G Global Navigator).

Inclines were reported on an average of various places on the slope when applicable.

Inclines were reported in this book in degrees. The following is a conversion chart for those desiring the same information reported in % grade.

Conversion of degrees to % grade
10 degrees is 18% grade
12 degrees is 21% grade
14 degrees is 25% grade
16 degrees is 29% grade
18 degrees is 32% grade
20 degrees is 36% grade
22 degrees is 40% grade

Formula: To convert degrees to % grade, use a calculator with a tangent function. Enter the number of degrees, then press the 'tan' button. For an approximation, double the degrees and the answer will be close to the % grade.

Trail hiking time frame

All trails in this book were hiked by at least one of the authors in the summer and fall of 2003. Conditions were reported as accurately as possible; however, conditions can change due to environmental factors. Improvements continue to be made on trails.

We advise you to call ahead to the respective trail headquarters for current conditions (phone numbers are provided after Inclines and Alerts on all hiking trails. When available, the North Country Trail Association posts conditions on their website at www.northcountrytrail.org).

Photography Credits

All photos were taken by the authors with a Nikon N80 (Tornabene), Olympus Camedia C-730 Digital (Morgan) and Canon EOS Elan 7E (Vogelsang).

APPENDIX D: BIBLIOGRAPHY
References used in writing this book

Ashland Chamber of Commerce & County Tourism. *Ashland & Bayfield County Visitor Guide.* Ashland, WI: Printing Plus/Screen Line, 2003.

Bayfield Chamber of Commerce. *Bayfield Vacation & Visitor Guide.* Merrill, WI: Reindl Printing, 2003.

Chronic Disease Prevention Committee. *Community Lakewalk: Ashland's Scenic Pathway to Health.* [Brochure], 2001.

Hansen, E. *Hiking Wisconsin: A Falcon Guide.* Guilford, CT: The Globe Pequot Press, 2002.

Hintz, M. *Hiking Wisconsin: America's Best Day Hiking Series.* Champaign, IL: Human Kinetics, 1997.

McGrath, W.C. *Great Wisconsin Walks: 45 Strolls, Rambles, Hikes, and Treks.* Black Earth, WI: Trails Books, 1997.

Tornabene, L., M. Morgan and L. Vogelsang. *Gentle Hikes: Minnesota's Most Scenic North Shore Hikes Under 3 Miles.* Cambridge, MN: Adventure Publications, Inc., 2002.

Wisconsin Department of Natural Resources. *Amnicon Falls State Park Geology Walk.* [Booklet], 2003.

Wisconsin Department of Natural Resources. *Amnicon Falls State Park Thimbleberry Nature Trail.* [Booklet], 2003.

Wisconsin Department of Natural Resources. *Big Bay State Park.* [Brochure], 2002.

Wisconsin Department of Natural Resources. *Brule River State Forest.* [Brochure], 2002.

Wisconsin Department of Tourism. *Osaugie Trail.* [Brochure].

Wisconsin Department of Natural Resources. *Pattison State Park Big Manitou Geology Walk.* [Booklet], 2000.

Wisconsin Department of Natural Resources. *State Park Visitor (Amnicon, Pattison & Copper Falls).* [Newspaper], 2003.

References for Hiking for Health and Says Who...

1. D. Schardt, "These Feet Were Made for Walking: Health Benefits of Walking and Other Moderate Exercise," *Nutrition Action Healthletter* 20, no.10 (Dec1993):4. **2.** R. Ross, J.A. Freeman, I. Janssen, "Exercise Alone Is an Effective Strategy for Reducing Obesity and Related Comorbidities," *Exercise and Sports Sciences Reviews* 28, no.4 (2000):165–170. **3.** J E Manson, F.B. Hu, J.W. Rich-Edwards and others, "A Prospective Study of Walking as Compared with Vigorous Exercise in the Prevention of Coronary Heart Disease in Women," *New England Journal of Medicine* 341, no. 9 (1999):650–658. **4.** A.A. Hakim, J.D. Curb, H. Petrovitch and others, "Effects of Walking on Coronary Heart Disease in Elderly Men: The Honolulu Heart Program," *Circulation* 100, no. 1 (1999): 9–13. **5.** K.E. Powell, K.D. Thompson, C.J. Casperson, J.S. Kendrick, "Physical Activity and the Incidence of Coronary Artery Disease," *Annual Review of Public Health* 8 (1987): 253–287. **6.** "Physical Activity,

Part II–Exercise: A Good Health Prescription," *Harvard Women's Health Watch* 8, no. 11 (Jul 2001):NA. **7.** F.B. Hu, M.J. Stampfer, G.A. Colditz and others, "Physical Activity and Risk of Stroke in Women," *Journal of the American Medical Association* 283, no. 2 (2000): 2961–67. **8.** Haskell et al, "Cardiovascular Benefits and Assessment of Physical Fitness in Adults," *Medicine and Science in Sports and Exercise* 26, no.6 (1992): S210–S220. **9.** J.J. Duncan, N.F. Gordon, C.B. Scott, "Women Walking for Health and Fitness: How Much is Enough?" *Journal of the American Medical Association* 266. no 23 (1991): 3295–99. **10.** A.H. Mokdad, B.A. Bowman, E.S. Ford, F. Vinicor, J.S. Marks, J.P. Koplan "The Continuing Epidemics of Obesity and Diabetes in the United States," *Journal of the American Medical Association* 286, no.10 (2001):1195–1200. **11.** Statistics related to overweight and obesity: NIDDK Weight Control and Information Network. NIH Fact Sheet No. 3-4158 July 2003 (e-text posted: July 03) (www.niddk.nih.gov/health/nutrit/pubs/statobes.htm) (accessed October 12, 2003). **12.** S.P. Helmrich, D.R. Raglund, R.S. Paffenbarger, Jr. "Prevention of Non-Insulin-Dependent Diabetes Mellitus with Physical Activity," *Medicine and Science in Sports and Exercise* 26 (1994): 824–830. **13.** H.E. Resnick, P. Valsania, J.B. Halter, X. Lin, "Relation of Weight Gain and Weight Loss on Subsequent Diabetes Risk in Overweight Adult,". *Journal of Epidemiology Community Health* 54 (2000):506–602. **14.** B.M. Massie, "Obesity and Heart Failure—Risk Factor or Mechanism?" *New England Journal of Medicine* 347, no.5 (2003):305–313. **15.** E.E. Calle, C. Rodriguez, K. Walker-Thurmond, M.J. Thun, "Overweight, Obesity, and Mortality from Cancer in a Prospectively Studied Cohort of U.S. Adults," *New England Journal of Medicine* 348, no.17 (2003):1625–38. **16.** R.L. Weinsier, G.R. Hunter, A.F. Heini, M.I. Goran, S.M Sell, "The Etiology of Obesity: Relative Contributions of Metabolic Factors, Diet, and Physical Exercise," *American Journal of Medicine* 105 (1998):145–150. **17.** B.E Ainsworth, W.L. Haskell, A.S. Leon, D.R. Jacobs Jr., H.J. Montove, J.F. Sallis, R.S. Paffenbarger Jr., *Compendium of Physical Activities: Classification of Energy Costs of Human Physical Activities, American College of Sports Medicine's Resource Manual for Guidelines for Exercise Testing and Prescription (4th Ed)*, (Philadelphia: Lippencott, Williams & Wilkins, 2001). **18.** R.J. Shephard, G.J. Balady, "Exercise as Cardiovascular Therapy," *Circulation* 99, no. 7 (1999):963–972. **19.** S. Percy, "Putting One Foot in Front of the Other: Walking for Exercise," *Harvard Health Letter* 22, no. 6 (Apr 1997): 2. **20.** W.C. Willet, "Balancing Lifestyle and Genomics Research for Disease Prevention," *Science* 296, no.5568 (2002):695–598. **21.** B. Liebman, "Fat Chance: Extra Pounds Can Increase Your Cancer Risk," *Nutrition Action Health Letter* Oct 30, no.8 (2003):1,3–6. **22.** "Physical Activity and Cardiovascular Health," *NIH Consensus Statement Online* 13, no.3 (December 18–20 1995):1–33 (accessed Sept. 24, 2003). **23.** K.J. Coleman, H.R. Raynor, D.M. Mueller and others, "Providing Sedentary Adults with Choices for Meeting Their Walking Goals," *Preventive Medicine* 28, no. 5 (1999): 510–519. **24.** E.R. Eichner, "Infection, Immunity and Exercise: What to Tell Patients," *The Physician and Sportsmedicine* 21 (1993):125–135. **25.** K.R. Fontain, "Physical Activity Improves Mental Health," *The Physician and Sportsmedicine* 28, no.10 (2000):83–83. **26.** B.G. Berger, D. Pargman, R.S. Weinberg, *Foundations of Exercise Psychology* (Morgantown, WV: Fitness Information Technology; 2002). **27.** K.F. Hays, *Working It Out: Using Exercise in Psychotherapy* (Washington, DC: American Psychological Association, 1999) **28.** S.T. Walters, J.E. Martin, "Does Aerobic Exercise Really Enhance Self Esteem in Children? A Prospective Evaluation in 3rd–5th Graders," *Journal of Sport Behavior* 23, no.1 (2000):51–60. **29.** A.F. Kramer, N.J. Hahn, M.T. Banich and others, "Ageing, Fitness and Neurocognitive Function," *Nature* 400, (1999): 418–19. **30.** S. Colcombe, A.F. Kramer, "Fitness Effects on the Cognitive Function of Older Adults: A Meta-Analytic Study," *Psychological Science* 14, no.2 (2003): 125–131. **31.** K. Yaffe, D. Barnes, M. Nevitt and others, "A Prospective Study of Physical Activity and Cognitive Decline in Elderly Women: Women Who Walk," *Archives of Internal Medicine* 161, no. 14 (2001): 1703–8. **32.** S. Colcombe, K.I. Erickson, N. Raz, A.G. Webb, N.J. Cohen, E. McAuley, A.F. Kramer, "Aerobic Fitness Reduces Brain Tissue Loss in Aging Humans," *Journals of Gerontology Series A: Biological Sciences & Medical Sciences* 58A, no.2 (2003):176–81. **33.** S. Brink, "Smart Moves: New Research Suggest that Folks from 8 to 80 Can Shape up Their Brains with Aerobic Exercise," *U.S. News & World Report* 118, no. 19 (May 15 1995) 76(6). **34.** B.H. Marcus, A.E. Albrecht, T.K. King, et al, "The Efficacy of Exercise as an Aid for Smoking Cessation in Women: A Randomized Controlled Trial," *Archives of Internal Medicine* 159 (1999):1229–1234. **35.** M.J. Cohen, *Reconnecting with Nature* (Corvallis, OR: Ecopress, 1997) **36.** D. Sharpe, *The Psychology of Color* (Chicago: Nelson-Hall 1974). **37.** T. Grill, M. Scanlon, *Photographic Composition* (New York: Amphoto 1990). **38.** D. Foltz-Gray, "Exercise in Romance: What's the Best Way to Renew Your Commitment to Fitness–and to Your Relationship? (Walking)" *Health* 15, no. 4 (2001): 48(3). **39.** J. McChesney, S. Knight, B. Boswell, M. Hamer, "Interrelatedness Between Recreational Activity and Spirituality: The Perspectives of Persons with Disabilities," *Research Quarterly for Exercise and Sport* 71, no. 1 (2000): Supplement: A-50. **40.** A. Bauman, "Running on Faith," *Runners World* 34, no. 6 (Jun 1999): 86 (1). **41.** S.G. Wannamethee, A.G. Shaper, M. Walker, "Physical Activity and Mortality in Older Men with Diagnosed Coronary Heart Disease," *Circulation* 102, no. 12 (2000): 1358–63. **42.** P. Seraganian, editor *Exercise Psychology: The Influence of Physical Exercise on Psychological Processes* (New York: John Wiley & Sons, 1993) **43.** L.M. Leith, *Foundations of Exercise and Mental Health* (Morgantown, WV: Fitness Information Technology, 1994) **44.** L.M. Leith, *Exercising Your Way to Better Mental Health* (Morgantown, WV: Fitness Information Technology, 1998) **45.** D.L. Drotar, "Reaching New Heights: Hiking Your Way to Physical and Mental Fitness," *American Fitness* 16, no. 3 (May–Jun 1998):48(3). **46.** M. Malecki, "Promoting Spiritual Wellness in Medical, Psychological and Other Health Care Settings: Assisting the Health Client to Access the Inner Healer," *Dissertation Abstracts International–Section B: The Sciences and Engineering* 56, no. 11-B (1996): 6030(190). **47.** M.I. Wallace, "The Wild Bird Who Heals: Recovering the Spirit in Nature," *Theology Today* 50, no. 1 (Apr 1993): 13(16). **48.** G.A. Kelly, K.S. Kelly, Z.V. Tran, "Walking and Resting Blood Pressure in Adults: A Meta-Analysis," *Preventive Medicine* 33 (2001): 120–127. **49.** "Hitting the Trail in Good Form," *Harvard Women's Health Letter* 7, no. 10 (June 2000): NA **50.** D.H. Passe, M. Horn, R. Murray, "Impact of Beverage Acceptability on Fluid Intake During Exercise," *Appetite* 35 (2000): 219–229. **51.** F. Sizer, E. Whitney, *Nutrition: Concepts and Controversies (8th edition)* (Belmont, CA: Wadsworth **52.** P. Knekt, J. Kumpulainen, R. Järvinen, H. Rissanen, M. Heliövaara, A. Reunanen, T. Hakulinen, A. Aromaa, "Flavonoid Intake and Risk of Chronic Diseases," *American Journal of Clinical Nutrition* 76, no.3 (2002):560–568.

GLOSSARY OF TERMS:

This is not a conclusive list; however, we have included terms that may not be familiar to our readers that were used in our trails, Almost Hikes, waysides and picnic areas.

Amenities: Indicates availability of such things as restrooms, water fountains, visitor centers, picnic tables, playgrounds, grills, shelters, boat launches, etc. Note: For clarity, we indicate restrooms by toilet type: flush (modern), vault (pit), portable (port-a-pottys, portalets).

Boardwalk: Long boards laid side by side or end to end, to make walking easier over a particular section. These may be slippery when wet or frosted; may be loose in some areas; may be difficult to use with hiking poles or challenging to navigate if narrow. Always use caution when crossing them.

Laid log paths: Sometimes referred to as cut-log paths, these are normally laid side by side across the trail to facilitate crossing a muddy section, are often unsecured or loose. These may be challenging to navigate regardless of conditions. Always use caution when crossing them.

Seasonal: Some of our trailhead facilities and amenities will have a seasonal notation. Seasonal is typically defined as the period of time from mid-May to mid-October. This being northern Wisconsin, these are close approximations based on ground freezing/thawing. Many of the waysides are closed during snow season as they are not plowed.

Spur Trail: A trail that connects to the main trail, typically leading to a point of interest or scenic overlook.

Universal Design Standards: Universal Design means that the trail meets accessibility standards for persons of all physical abilities.

Wheelchair accessible: We have used this term throughout the book regarding parking and other amenities. It is defined as a location that can be accessed by someone using a wheelchair. All flush toilets are wheelchair accessible. Accessibility of vault toilets varies, but most have handrails. Surfaces leading to vault toilets are typically hardpacked dirt and gravel. None of the portable toilets meet the criteria for wheelchair accessibility except at Billings Park.

CHECKLIST (USE THE BOXES TO CHECK THE TRAILS YOU'VE HIKED!)

TRAILS

Superior

- ☐ Millennium Trail (East)
- ☐ Millennium Trail (West)
- ☐ Riverfront Trail
- ☐ Barker's Island Trail
- ☐ Osaugie Trail: Superior Bay to Trail Beginning
- ☐ Osaugie Trail: Superior Bay to Old Stockade Site
- ☐ Osaugie Trail: Old Stockade Site to Loonsfoot Landing
- ☐ Big Manitou Falls Geology Walk
- ☐ Beaver Slide Nature Trail
- ☐ Dog Trail
- ☐ Little Falls Hiking Trail

Superior to Hurley on U.S. 2

- ☐ Amnicon Falls Geology Walk
- ☐ Amnicon Falls Picnic Stroll
- ☐ Thimbleberry Nature Trail
- ☐ Stony Hill Nature Trail
- ☐ Historical Bayfield Road Trail
- ☐ Marengo River Trail
- ☐ Boardwalk Trail East Loop
- ☐ Boardwalk Trail West Loop
- ☐ Artesian Way
- ☐ Cedar Edge Loop
- ☐ Marsh View Walk
- ☐ Ashland Bayfront Trail: Maslowski Beach to Hot Pond
- ☐ Ashland Bayfront Trail: Hot Pond to Reiss Coal Dock
- ☐ Ashland Bayfront Trail: Memorial Park to Krehar Park
- ☐ Ashland Bayfront Trail: Krehar Park to Water Plant
- ☐ Ashland Bayfront Trail: Bayview Park
- ☐ Three Brides Trail
- ☐ Observation Tower
- ☐ Red Granite Falls Trail
- ☐ Morgan Falls
- ☐ Potato River Upper Falls
- ☐ Potato River Lower Falls

Superior to Ashland on WI 13

- ☐ Winter Green/Top Ridge Trail
- ☐ Point Trail/Loop (South)
- ☐ Point Trail/Loop (North)
- ☐ Bay View Trail
- ☐ Boardwalk Interpretive Trail
- ☐ Lagoon Ridge Trail
- ☐ Big Bay Town Park Trail
- ☐ Casper Trail

Superior to Ashland on WI 13 (continued)

- ☐ Iron Bridge and Nature Trail
- ☐ Hauser Orchards "A-Peeling" Stroll
- ☐ Brownstone Trail North
- ☐ Brownstone Trail South
- ☐ Washburn Walking Trail
- ☐ Washburn Walking Trail (Wheelchair Accessible Section)
- ☐ Long Lake Trail
- ☐ Twin Lakes Trail

ALMOST HIKES
Superior

- ☐ Rhonda & Joe's Wedding Stroll
- ☐ Welcome-A-Board-Walk
- ☐ Wisconsin Point Lighthouse
- ☐ Superior Entry
- ☐ Big Manitou Falls
- ☐ Little Manitou Falls

Superior to Hurley on U.S. 2

- ☐ Amnicon Falls Wooded and Riverview Stroll
- ☐ Brule River View
- ☐ Northern Great Lakes Visitor Center Indoor Outing
- ☐ Prentice Park Wooded Stroll
- ☐ Prentice Park Promenade (East)
- ☐ Prentice Park Promenade (West)
- ☐ Penokee Scenic Overlook
- ☐ Loon Lake Beach Area
- ☐ Superior Falls
- ☐ Upson Falls

Superior to Ashland on WI 13

- ☐ Shoreline Cliffs and Inland Woods
- ☐ Port Wing Boreal Forest
- ☐ Iron Bridge Almost Hike
- ☐ Hauser's Superior View
- ☐ Superior Overlook at Big Bay State Park
- ☐ Big Bay Point
- ☐ Barrier Beach
- ☐ Big Bay Town Park Lagoon
- ☐ Not-To-Be Missed Panoramic Bay Stroll
- ☐ Long Lake Picnic Stroll

WAYSIDES AND SCENIC LOCALES
Superior

- ☐ Old Stockade Site Wayside

Superior to Hurley on U.S. 2

- ☐ Northwest Portal of Wisconsin Wayside
- ☐ Brule River Wayside
- ☐ Iron River Wayside
- ☐ Overlook Park Wayside
- ☐ Memorial Park Wayside
- ☐ Historical Marker of the Bad River
- ☐ Apostle Islands Scenic Overlook
- ☐ Gogebic Iron Range Wayside
- ☐ Wisconsin Travel Information Center

Superior to Ashland on WI 13

- ☐ Jardine Creek Wayside
- ☐ Old School Memorial Park
- ☐ Siskiwit Bay Park & Wayside

PICNIC AREAS
Superior

- ☐ Barker's Island Picnic Area
- ☐ Barker's Island Play Area Picnic Area
- ☐ Billings Park Picnic Area
- ☐ Bear Creek Park
- ☐ Big Manitou Falls Picnic Area
- ☐ Pattison State Park Main Picnic Area
- ☐ Little Manitou Falls Picnic Area

Superior to Hurley on U.S. 2

- ☐ Amnicon Falls State Park Sheltered Picnic Area
- ☐ Amnicon Falls State Park Accessible Picnic Area
- ☐ Bois Brule Picnic Area
- ☐ Prentice Park Picnic Area
- ☐ Maslowski Beach Picnic Area
- ☐ Krehar Park Picnic Area
- ☐ Copper Falls State Park Main Picnic Area
- ☐ Bayview Park Picnic Area
- ☐ Saxon Harbor Picnic Area

Superior to Ashland on WI 13

- ☐ Mouth of the Brule River Picnic Area
- ☐ Barrier Beach Picnic Area
- ☐ Big Bay Point Picnic Area
- ☐ Big Bay Town Park Picnic Area
- ☐ Memorial Park/Joni's Beach Picnic Area
- ☐ Thompson's West End Picnic Area
- ☐ Long Lake Picnic Area

INDEX

ABOUT THE AUTHORS

Trails of a "Champ"-ion

To support health education majors in pursuing their passion, Ladona Tornabene has started the Trails of a "Champ"-ion Scholarship Fund through the University of Minnesota Duluth. A portion of the proceeds from the sale of this book go to that scholarship fund.

From left to right, Ladona Tornabene, Champ (UMD's mascot), Melanie Morgan, Lisa Vogelsang

About the Authors

Ladona Tornabene, Ph.D., CHES is an Assistant Professor of Health Education and Certified Health Education Specialist at the University of Minnesota Duluth. Her focus lies in confronting the number one public health problem in America today—lack of physical activity. This fact, combined with what she knows about nature's ability to reduce stress, fueled a passion. That passion is to promote better health through opening the outdoors to people of all abilities. She believes the marvelous scenery that Lake Superior's south shore and northern Wisconsin boasts is prime incentive for accomplishing such a mission. Though an advocate for active lifestyles, she desires for people to know that health is more than just being in good physical shape. Health has a psychological, social, environmental and spiritual dimension as well. Her advice? For better health on the inside—Get outside!

Melanie Morgan's organizational skills and attention to detail were instrumental to the completion of this book. She may be a Minnesota native, but over the years she has spent considerable time driving the back roads of Wisconsin visiting relatives and the old places with her parents, both of whom were born and raised in small, rural Wisconsin towns. Exploring those old haunts and farms with cousins always led to exciting times and expanded her adventurous spirit. Melanie and her husband, Mark, enjoy hiking and snowshoeing in the woods out the back door of their rural Duluth home.

Lisa Vogelsang, Ph.D. is an assistant professor (part-time) at the College of St. Scholastica in Duluth, Minnesota teaching Psychology and American Sign Language (ASL). Additionally, she is a certified massage therapist who developed the Massage Therapy Program at Duluth Business University and remains a consultant for the program. A former two-time Olympian, she loves the outdoors, especially Lake Superior and the shores around it. Lisa enjoys photography, hiking, biking, sea kayaking, cross country skiing and snowshoeing. After five ankle surgeries and developing severe ankle arthritis from a previous athletic injury, she must keep her hikes short and less rugged. Her disability was, in part, a catalyst in the conception of this and the previous book, *Gentle Hikes: Minnesota's Most Scenic North Shore Hikes Under 3 Miles.*

For more information and additional pictures from both Gentle Hikes (Minnesota and Wisconsin) books, or to let the authors know what you think of either book, please visit the Gentle Hikes website at www.d.umn.edu/~ltornabe/gh